Derbyshire
MURDERS

Derbyshire
MURDERS

MARTIN BAGGOLEY

The
History
Press

This book is dedicated to my old friend,
David Stubbings.

First published 2008

The History Press Ltd
The Mill, Brimscombe Port
Stroud, Gloucestershire, GL5 2QG
www.thehistorypress.co.uk

Reprinted in 2009

British Library Cataloguing in Publication Data.
A catalogue record for this book is available from the British Library.

ISBN 978 0 7509 4507 3

Typesetting and origination by The History Press Ltd.
Printed in Great Britain

CONTENTS

ACKNOWLEDGEMENTS

I would like to thank the staff at the British Newspaper Library at Colindale and at Derby Local Studies Library. I am grateful to Amy Goodwin at Buxton Museum, and to Jackie Ledder and Geoff Parker for their help with the illustrations. The support given to me by the staff at the Ramsbottom branch of The Royal Bank of Scotland has been invaluable. Thanks also to my editor, Matilda Richards, at The History Press.

1

A CRIME OF COMMON PURPOSE

Stanley, 1842

Seventy-year-old Martha Goddard lived with her sister Sarah, who was four years her junior, at the secluded Stanley Hall, six miles from Derby. It was a large residence, 100 yards from their closest neighbours, surrounded by orchards and fields, and which was approached by a private road.

The daughters of a former vicar of Tideswell, the Misses Goddard, as they were affectionately known throughout the district, had never married. They were members of one of the county's most respectable and wealthiest families. They were noted for being charitable, kind and humane, but they also had a reputation for being rather eccentric. Fiercely independent, they lived alone and had no permanent servants. If any work needed to be done to the Hall or in the garden, the sisters hired local people from the village of Stanley. By the autumn of 1842, they had lived under the same roof for more than forty years.

Their isolated location and independent nature meant that they were vulnerable, and they had been the victims of two burglaries already that year. In April, two men had broken into their home, and, after threatening Martha, the culprits escaped with several articles of silver and a number of sovereigns.

In early September, a second burglary had occurred and several pieces of linen were taken. However, the sisters had not been disturbed, and had only become aware of the crime when they awoke the next morning. Following this, their friends attempted to persuade them to employ two live-in servants, to offer at least some protection. However, Martha and Sarah would not agree to such a suggestion, and continued to live on their own as they had for many years previously.

However, the concern for their well being, which had been shown by their friends, proved to have been well founded. At 5 a.m. on Friday, 30 September 1842, their neighbours, Mr and Mrs Scattergood, woke to the sound of Sarah hammering at their door. She was in great distress and her nightdress was covered in blood, for she had been the victim of a vicious assault. She told the Scattergoods that another burglary had occurred, that both she and her sister had been attacked, and she believed Martha to have been murdered.

The Scattergoods alerted other neighbours Mr and Mrs Hartson, and together they all made their way to the Hall, which they discovered to have been ransacked. They found Martha in her bedroom, lying on her back on the bed, her legs protruding over the side and resting on a chair. Her eyes were closed, but she was still breathing, albeit with great difficulty. Unable to speak, she was covered in blood and there was a great quantity on the bed and on the floor.

Dr Robert Boden of Smalley arrived at 7 a.m. and found Martha insensible but clinging to life. Tragically, however, she died thirty minutes later. The doctor found four severe wounds to her head, each of which was 1¾in long, and three of these had resulted in fractures to the skull, and these had been the cause of death. All had probably been caused by the same weapon, which he thought was a type of iron bar. He also confirmed that it had been used with considerable force against the elderly victim.

Other injuries included considerable bruising to the right side of her neck, a wound to her left wrist and left forefinger, bruising to the back of her left hand, and the ring finger of her right hand was fractured.

Dr Boden treated Sarah's injuries at the scene, which, although serious, were not life threatening. There was bruising to her face, neck and hands; he found two wounds on the left side of her head, and the middle finger of her left hand was fractured. He concluded that Sarah's injuries had been caused by a similar weapon to that which had been used against her sister.

The police discovered a ladder leaning against the wall of the coalhouse, which was about 7ft high. Several tiles had been removed from the coalhouse roof, creating a hole large enough for a man to lower himself through. Once inside the coalhouse the intruders had passed through a door into the kitchen, from which another door led into the main living area of the Hall.

Sarah told the police that the intruders demanded to be shown where their cash and valuables were kept. They took two sovereigns and a few shillings, together with several shawls, a yellow handkerchief, a brown apron and several pieces of cloth, but missed two £5 notes.

The inquest into Martha's death was held at the White Hart in Stanley before the coroner, Henry Mozley. The jury heard evidence from the neighbours who responded to Sarah's pleas for help, and medical evidence given by Dr Boden. Additionally, they heard Sarah's own account of what had occurred. She told the court:

> On Thursday night last, my sister went to bed about ten o' clock. I sat up a great deal later. About half past twelve o'clock on Friday morning, I was sitting by the fire in the house place, and heard a noise like mortar falling. The sound came from the coalhouse, the door of which was open. Just as I got to it there came out of it two men who knocked me down, and afterwards went up to my sister's room. When I was able to get up again, I went upstairs to my room, and the men came into it, and knocked me down again with heavy iron bars they had in their hands. They were very stern savage men. They stayed in the house about ninety minutes, and they then left it. Soon after they had gone I went into my sister's room and found her lying, bleeding, on her back across the bed. I put her legs on a chair and alarmed the neighbours. When I first went in my sister said to me, 'Sally! Sally! A man! A man!' and she moaned. I cannot describe the men.

The inquest jury returned a verdict of wilful murder, and a reward of £100 was offered immediately by Martha's friends for information leading to the arrest of those responsible for the crime. A few days later the Home Secretary agreed to an additional reward of £100, which included an offer to pardon any participant in the crime, if not the actual murderer, who would identify those responsible and give evidence against them on behalf of the Crown. Within twenty-four hours of the murder being committed, two local villains named Keeling and Green had fallen under suspicion and were arrested. However, it was soon established that they had not been responsible. They were released after the police received information implicating three other men in the crime, all of whom were known criminals.

News of the murder had broken during the early hours of Friday – market day in Derby – and the crime at Stanley Hall was the day's major topic of conversation. One of those who returned home at the end of the day's business was Joseph Simpson, a needle maker from the village of Heage. That evening he discussed the case with his neighbour, John Hulme. During their conversation, Hulme blurted out that he had been one of the burglars, and telling Simpson, 'I'll go and tell Bonsall, and he must tell Bland. Nobody can swear to us as nobody was there.'

The following night Hulme met a friend, known as Domino, for a drink. Domino knew that Hulme had taken part in the two earlier burglaries of Stanley Hall, and raised the matter of the murder with him. Hulme admitted that he had been present when Martha was beaten, but

The gable end of Stanley Hall and the coalhouse, through which the murderers gained entry. (The Derby & Chesterfield Reporter and Derbyshire Chronicle)

insisted that he had not been responsible for her death. He again named his accomplices as Samuel Bonsall and William Bland, adding that Bonsall had committed the murder.

With a reward of £200 on offer, Hulme was clearly being naïve in believing that his admitting to having taken part in the crime would not be reported to the authorities. Domino contacted Constable John Hawkins, who immediately arranged for the houses of the three men to be searched. At Bonsall's home, a quantity of items including a flannel shirt were found; at Bland's home, a brown apron was discovered hidden away. It was later established that all of these items had been taken from Stanley Hall on the night of the crime. At this stage, nothing was found in Hulme's house, but Joseph Simpson, with the assistance of Richard Dronsfield, a youngster apprenticed to Hulme, would later uncover a large quantity of the items stolen from Stanley Hall, which had been buried by Hulme.

John Hulme. (The Derby & Chesterfield Reporter and Derbyshire Chronicle)

Bonsall and Bland were arrested and brought before Sarah. She did not recognise Bland, but she identified Bonsall, saying, 'He was the man who looked stern and savage at me, and shook his fist. He also knocked me down and afterwards beat me with an iron bar.'

Hulme meanwhile had fled the area, and a reward of £50 was offered for his capture. He travelled to his hometown of Leek in Staffordshire, where his parents still lived. After a few days, during which he had remained hidden, he contacted them through an intermediary, and his mother and father assured him that it was safe to come to the house. However, they had contacted their local constable, and he was arrested as soon as he entered the family home. All three suspects were now in custody.

Twenty-four-year-old John Hulme, also known as Holme, Starbuck and Jack the Sweep, had left his parents' home when he was eleven years old. He was apprenticed to a chimneysweep and travelled the countryside using this employment as a cover for finding houses to break into. Two of his brothers had already been transported for crimes they had committed. Samuel Bonsall, also known as Bonser, was twenty-six years old, and William Bland was aged thirty-nine. Both men were colliers, originally natives of Belper, and were known burglars.

Their trial took place on Monday, 20 March 1843, and at 7 a.m. the courtroom was already packed. Many were locked out and some of these climbed on to the roof of the court building to watch the proceedings through the rooftop windows. At 9 a.m. the trial judge, Mr Justice Gurney, took his seat and the hearing began.

The prosecution was conducted by Mr Clarke, Mr Whitehurst and Mr Fowler. Bonsall was represented by Mr Miller, but Hulme and Bland had no legal representation. The statements made by Hulme and Bland contained admissions that they had taken part in the crime, but each man attempted to distance himself from the actual murder. Unlike his co-accused, Bonsall denied any involvement and insisted he was not at the scene when the crime was committed. Each of the accused was hoping that if his version of events was accepted by the jury, he would perhaps avoid the noose.

Sarah Goddard was too distressed to attend the trial, and her identification evidence of Bonsall was therefore not presented to the jury. Nevertheless, the Crown was convinced it had a strong case against him and proceeded without her testimony.

William Bland's account, which formed the basis of his defence at the trial, had been taken down by the police following his arrest. It had been read out in the presence of his two co-accused on 21 October, and in it he stated that:

> I am innocent of the charge of wilful [*sic*] murder; I am innocent of that crime. I was there but on the outside. I mean on the outside of the buildings where the lady lived. Samuel Bonsall began to take the slates off and gave them me. This John Sweep as they call him, he goes by the name of John Starbuck, said, 'Damn you, stand on one side and let me take the slates off'. There was a bit of a ladder to get up to them. John Starbuck said, 'They have nailed a piece of wood on here since we were here before.' Samuel Bonsall goes up the ladder and pulled it off. And Samuel came down and the Sweep went up the ladder and went through. As soon as he got through, the maiden lady I think was nigh at hand. We went in the door. The Sweep unbolted it and said, 'Damn her eyes, I had to knock her over before I could unbolt the door'. He unbolted it – that is John Starbuck did, in the inside, and I and Bonsall went in. This was through the outer kitchen door. Samuel Bonsall and John Starbuck drove the lady upstairs. I did not offer to go up. John Starbuck said if I did not come up he would come and knock my

William Bland. (The
Derby & Chesterfield
Reporter and
Derbyshire Chronicle)

brains out. They damned and buggered me several times, and I was forced
to go up or else I was afraid for my life. Samuel Bonsall and John Starbuck
were plundering – that is throwing things on to the landing. John Starbuck
got this iron crow and said if I did not put the things into the bag he would
knock my brains out. They broke several chests open. They broke the door
open where this lady was. They got both their crowbars and sprung the
door open. The old lady, her as they killed, screamed out several times,
'Sally, come Sally!' Samuel Bonsall struck this old lady several times over
the ribs on the side. She kept screaming out like, and he struck her over
the head at last. He says, 'Damn you, I think I have cranked you at last'.
I don't know as I have anything more to say. The other old woman they said
was coming out, 'Damn her, stop her.' We were going back towards Heage
and met a man near some houses in a lane, which I understood Joseph Roe
to say this morning was Woodhouse Lane. I don't know justly the words
he said. He said, 'I think you have got something that is not your own'.

Samuel Bonsall.
(The Derby &
Chesterfield
Reporter and
Derbyshire
Chronicle)

Us three, Samuel Bonsall, John Starbuck and me met this man. John Starbuck says, 'You must be thankful you are against these houses or else we should have cranked you.' And Samuel Bonsall said, 'Never mind him, come on.' We went right home. They said there was 19*s* 6*d*, which they found on the premises, and they gave me 6*s* 6*d* of it. I have rather overrun my tale; John Starbuck says the old lady soon delivered up 6*s* 6*d*. That was all she had she said, and 13*s* Samuel Bonsall found, that made 19*s* 6*d*, they told me.

John Hulme's defence was given in the account which had been taken down in written form when he appeared before Leek Magistrates' Court, shortly after his arrest. It read as follows:

On Thursday, the night of the murder of Miss Goddard, Samuel Bonsall of Heage, a collier, came to see me at my house at Heage, in John Roger's Row, about 8 o'clock at night, where I was getting my supper. My wife and her mother were present. He asked me if I would go with him to Stanley about nine miles off Heage. I asked him what for and he answered to get some money.

He said there was plenty there, and I then said I would go with him. My wife and her mother were present and heard what passed. He then left my house and said he was going to William Bland's house near the barracks, and about five minutes after he came back with Bland to my house. We all set off directly. When we got to Miss Goddard's house, Samuel Bonsall took the slates off the low part of the building, a place where lumber and coal are kept. Samuel Bonsall then entered the place through the roof. I followed Bonsall through the hole. We let Bland in at the back door. It was bolted at top and bottom with wooden bolts. One of the ladies was gone to bed, the other was sitting up. Samuel Bonsall ill-used the lady that was sitting up, by striking her. This was in the kitchen. I could see what was passing by the light from the house place. She made her escape from him, and ran up the stairs. He followed her. She had locked the door; he prised the door open and demanded her money. I was then at the top of the stairs, and Bland was at the bottom. She gave Bonsall two sovereigns and some silver. Bonsall struck a light with a lucifer match and I saw the sovereigns and silver in his hand. Bonsall asked her if that was all the money she had, and said if she did not find more he would cut her throat, and at the same time drew a knife out of his pocket, one with a narrow pointed blade. I told Bonsall not to do any murder, but to come out of the room. He then came out and shut the door with the lady in. Bonsall then entered a room by bursting it open with a crowbar, opposite the one he had left. There was a lady in bed. I heard her shriek and Bonsall then ran towards her and knocked her brains out with a crowbar. I saw Bonsall give her the blow, he had the crowbar in one hand, and a candle in the other. The lady was just putting her feet on the floor at the time she was struck, and she fell on the floor. We then quitted the house all together. Bonsall took some calico and linen and put them in a sack, which he brought from his own house. We saw no more of the other lady. Bland was about three yards from me and I was at a distance not so far again from Bonsall when he struck the blow. We did not meet anybody either going or returning. The murder was committed between twelve and one o'clock at night. Bonsall, when he heard of the murder being made public on the Saturday night, told me that he should bury the calico and linen. I went home with Bonsall after the murder. We got there between four and five o'clock in the morning. Bonsall's wife was sitting up. I stopped at Bonsall's about ten minutes and then went home. I had 14s for my share of the money.

Despite the absence of a formal statement by Bonsall, the Crown had evidence provided by two prisoners who had shared a cell with him following his arrival at Derby Gaol in early October. These were William Salt, who at the time was imprisoned for not complying with a bastardy order, and John Brown, who was awaiting trial for the theft of a cow.

According to his two fellow prisoners, Bonsall told them that Hulme had called at his house on the night of the crime, and asked if he was interested in committing a burglary at Stanley. Bonsall's wife protested at the idea and told him, 'No my lad, go thee to bed'. Bonsall suggested that they rob a local tanner's yard instead, as he knew a shoemaker in Belper who would buy any leather they could get hold of. Hulme, however, was not interested in this idea, and finally Bonsall agreed to go with him to Stanley.

At Hulme's suggestion they called on Bland to ask if he wished to accompany them, and he readily agreed. The three men set off at 7 p.m. and arrived at Stanley Hall three hours later. Hulme was said to have removed the roof slates, and, on entering the house, he was confronted by Sarah, holding a poker in one hand and a candle in the other. Hulme knocked her down, and did so for a second time when she attempted to stand up.

Bonsall continued by insisting that Hulme and Bland forced Sarah upstairs, where they ransacked her bedroom, finding 12s 6d in one of the drawers. Bonsall later followed them and found Sarah screaming at Hulme, 'Man, man, what a man you are! I've given you my money. Tell me what you want and I will give it to you.' Hulme shouted back, 'You damned old woman. I want one of those £5 notes!', and he knocked her to the floor once again.

Meanwhile, Bland had burst into Martha's bedroom, with Bonsall supposedly exhorting him not to harm her in any way. At this point, Bonsall claimed he went downstairs to eat some cheese he had seen in the kitchen, leaving his two accomplices with the sisters. He returned upstairs some time later, having finished his meal, and on reaching Martha's room he heard Hulme say, 'I think we have nearly finished her, and now we'll go'.

Bonsall described his own weapon as a poker with a turned up tip; Hulme's was a strong piece of iron; and Bland's was a piece of wood lined with lead. He told Salt and Brown that all three weapons had been buried and would never be found.

Joseph Roe, a farmer who lived at Smalley Mill, was in Woodhouse Lane at 2.30 a.m. on the morning of the murder. He testified that he met the three accused, travelling from the direction of Stanley, heading towards Heage, which was about three miles from the spot where they met. Each of the men was carrying a bundle over his shoulder. Suspicious, Joseph said, 'Hullo my lads, have you got fighting cocks in your bags?' Bonsall, who Joseph knew, replied, 'What do you say?' Joseph suggested that they had been up to no good, as he was convinced they had stolen goods in their bundles.

Bonsall said to his two companions, 'Let's kill the bastard!' A defiant Joseph retorted, 'Come on, come on then!' Bonsall took a few paces towards him, but Bland called out, 'Oh come away, we have done enough for tonight'.

Another prosecution witness, Elizabeth Wainwright, who lived in Heage, also provided important evidence. She lived only a few yards from Bland's house, and could see if his door was open. On the night of 29 September she saw Bonsall arrive, and later noticed the three accused leave the house and make their way out of the village in the direction of Stanley. Importantly, having risen from her bed early in the morning to see her son off to work, she also saw the three men arrive back at the house several hours later, at about four o'clock.

Seventeen-year-old Richard Dronsfield was employed as an apprentice chimneysweep by Hulme, and lived in his employer's house. He testified that on that same evening, Bonsall called at the house and he heard him ask Hulme, 'Are you ready?' Hulme finished his supper after which the two men left. He saw Hulme put a bag and two short staves in his pockets, together with a knife he had made out of a razor. The youngster could also see that Bonsall had brought an iron crowbar with him.

Richard slept on the floor downstairs, and was woken by the two men when they returned in the early hours of the following morning. The fire was still lit and the youngster could see that Hulme's bag was full of various items. He and Bonsall examined their clothes for blood, and having found some they wiped it off. Richard could also see that Bonsall had blood on his left hand.

Richard saw Hulme empty his bag, which contained two shawls, some stockings and other items of clothing. There were several pieces of material, and he heard Hulme say, 'This will make thee and me some waistcoats'. He also heard him say that he thought one of the shawls might be worth as much as 30s. Having thrown the staves into the fire, Bonsall left the house.

At six o'clock that morning, Richard left to sweep a chimney, and when he returned a few hours later, he found the three accused at the house. Hulme led the other two to the door, saying, 'Its all clear, you may go now'. Bonsall returned the following day, and he and Hulme decided to bury the proceeds of the crime in the garden of a neighbour, John Rogers.

Upon hearing of the arrest of his two accomplices, Hulme took Richard to the garden where the booty was buried, and moved it, apparently worried lest Bonsall tell the police where it was, thus incriminating him in the crime. The pair then travelled to Leek and on the journey Hulme admitted to his apprentice that he had taken part in the burglary, but insisted that Bonsall and Bland had killed Martha.

After hearing of Hulme's arrest, Richard wandered the countryside, worried lest he be considered a suspect. He eventually returned to Heage several weeks later, where he contacted Joseph Simpson. The two of them retrieved the proceeds of the crime that had been reburied by Hulme and took them to Constable Hawkins. These proved to be valuable items of prosecution evidence, as neighbours and friends identified them as having belonged to the Goddard sisters. Importantly, they also confirmed that they had seen them in the sisters' possession after the two earlier burglaries that year, so the items could only have been taken on the night of the murder. Far from being considered a suspect, Richard was viewed as a crucial Crown witness, and so he proved to be at the trial.

Although it did not link Bonsall directly to the crime, further damning evidence was provided by a fellow prisoner, Benjamin Potter, who was in Derby Gaol awaiting trial for police assault. Given his status as a prisoner facing trial for a capital offence, Bonsall was not permitted to send any uncensored mail out of the gaol. He therefore attempted to gain Potter's assistance in smuggling a letter out to his father, written on a page torn from a Bible, obviously in the hope of establishing an alibi; it read:

> You must get Varges in come and sware he saw me stand in the yard in my short pising as I was going to call Abraham Jackson to go to work and I asked him what o clock it was, and he said it was about two, and olievar was in the little house and he asked me if I was going to work and I said I was not. It was about half past one I was doing a job for myself in the garding before the door. I was in my shirt. You must let me know if they will come.

Unfortunately for Bonsall, the letter was discovered by an alert assistant turnkey, Edward White, and it never reached its intended destination.

After the final witness had left the stand, Bonsall's lawyer, Mr Miller, suggested to the jury that the witnesses for the Crown had been motivated by financial gain as they had their sights set on the substantial reward and should be ignored. Other evidence had been given by criminals and therefore could not be trusted. As for the attempt to arrange a false alibi, he believed it was not significant as it was simply the act of an innocent man desperate to extricate himself from a nightmarish situation.

In his summing up, the judge highlighted the evidence that placed all three men together shortly before and immediately after the crime. As for the matter of the false alibi, the jury must decide for themselves what significance they put on it. He emphasised that the jury did not have to decide which individual had actually struck the blows that killed Martha. If they were satisfied that each of the prisoners in the dock had armed himself, and that they were acting with a common purpose, each was equally guilty of the murder, irrespective of who had struck the fatal blows.

The jury retired for a little over ten minutes before returning, having found all three defendants guilty of wilful murder. The judge passed death sentences on them and concluded by saying, 'May God Almighty have mercy on your guilty souls', to which Bonsall shouted, 'There is no God!'

The prisoners were taken down into the cells, but there was one more case to be heard before the close of the day's proceedings. John Brown was brought into the dock, but no evidence was offered against him relating to the theft of a cow, and he was released.

The executions took place at noon on Friday, 31 March 1843, the scaffold having been erected during the previous week, on top of the water tank to the left of the gaol's main gate. Derby had not witnessed an execution since John Leedham was hanged for bestiality on 12 April 1833, and inevitably a triple hanging was bound to generate widespread interest. The crowd, which had begun to arrive from all over the county in the early hours of the morning, was estimated to be more than 50,000.

Inside the gaol, the condemned men prepared themselves for what lay ahead. At 9 a.m. all of the gaol's inmates attended divine service in the chapel, at which Revd G. Pickering read the special service for the condemned. He and Revd Vevers, a Wesleyan Methodist minister, remained with the three men throughout the morning.

At a few minutes before noon the Under Sheriff, Mr Simpson, accompanied by a number of javelin men, arrived at the gaol to make his formal request that the condemned men be placed in his custody. As they left the condemned cell, the procession passed through the prison yard, in which a number of prisoners had gathered. Bonsall cried out, 'God bless you lads. Take warning lads, take warning!'

They were pinioned just before stepping out onto the scaffold, and Bonsall was the first to emerge before the vast crowd. His chest was heaving violently, his eyes were sunken and his face was pallid. Bland was the next to emerge, appearing relatively calm, but deep in prayer. Hulme could be seen to be trembling, and he too was praying as he stepped on to the drop. As the caps were drawn over their heads, the three men raised their voices in prayer, seeking forgiveness. The bolt was drawn and all three struggled for about two minutes before they finally became still. They were cut down one hour later, after which local sculptor W. Barton made death masks of each one.

In addition, Manchester phrenologist, Mr Ball, had been commissioned to make phrenological measurements of the men. The so-called science of phrenology was seen as a means of assessing an individual's character and intelligence from the shape of his or her skull. The skulls of criminals, especially those guilty of capital crimes, were regularly measured in the hope of finding ways of identifying those that posed a threat to society.

Crowds at public executions were notoriously raucous, but on this occasion the spectators were well behaved throughout the day. However, that evening more than 1,500 people, many the worse for drink, struggled to find seats on the special trains that had been laid on to bring them to Derby from many of the surrounding towns and villages for the hangings earlier in the day, and which would take them home that evening. Fighting broke out, but the police eventually managed to restore order.

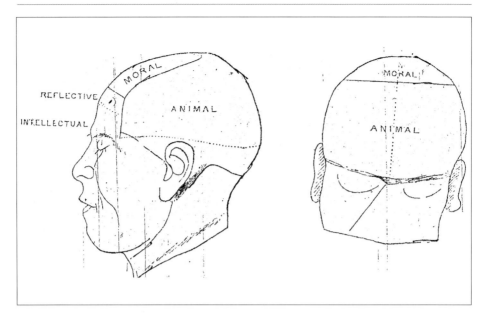

Hulme's head and broad thick neck exhibited large animal propensities. Amativeness, secretiveness, acquisitiveness, destructiveness and combativeness were very largely developed. In the moral sentiment portion, firmness is large, benevolence moderate, while hope, conscientiousness and ideality are small. The forehead was low and conical in shape, indicating an absence of mirth and ideality. As for his temperament, this was described as bilious, lymphatic and sanguine but essentially obstinate, gross, tyrannical, cunning, and was considered to be capable of murder. (The Derby & Chesterfield Reporter and Derbyshire Chronicle)

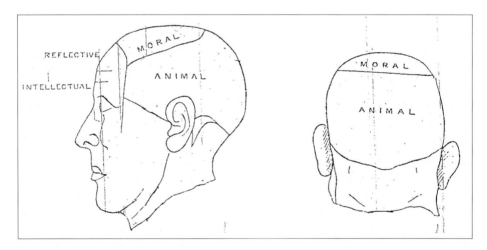

Mr Ball found that Bland's measurements confirmed that in his head the moral sentiments were the best of the three criminals, but were still relatively low. In the intellectual portion of the brain, the forehead showed more reflection and ideality than the others. Education, he conceded, might have been of some benefit upon an individual possessing such characteristics. (The Derby & Chesterfield Reporter and Derbyshire Chronicle)

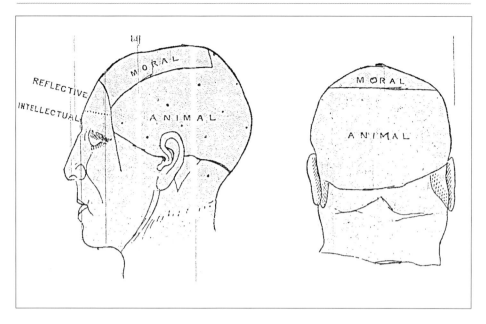

The phrenological drawing of Samuel Bosnall's head, in which the animal portion of the brain was large, the moral portion low and narrow, and the intellectual portion was small. Measurements taken with callipers denote the organs of veneration, hope, conscientiousness and ideality as being small, but those of secretiveness, destructiveness, acquisitiveness and amativeness are extremely large. Bonsall's temperament was described as lymphatic and sanguine with a small portion of biliousness. (The Derby & Chesterfield Reporter and Derbyshire Chronicle)

Revd Vevers had been asked to visit Bland, and after doing so, the other two condemned men asked him to visit them also. He called at the prison as often as four times each day, and at these meetings he was pleased to minister to their spiritual needs. However, this was not before he had made it clear to each man that he believed them all to be guilty, and that they deserved to hang. On the Monday following the executions, he held a public meeting at the Wesleyan Chapel on King Street, at which he addressed a packed hall on his meetings with the murderers of Martha Goddard.

He described their emotional farewells to families and friends. Although greatly distressed, Hulme said goodbye to his wife stoically. Bland wept openly as he spoke to his children through the prison bars, unable to embrace them. Bonsall's brother made to leave after his visit, and as he did so they shook hands through the bars of the cell, but they did not release their grip for more than ten minutes; Bonsall wept continuously, until, regaining his composure, he told his brother, 'Now my lad, keep out of the public house, and give over the cards and dice, for they are the foundations of all misery.'

Revd Vevers next told of a dramatic meeting in the gaol's schoolroom with the three men on the morning of their executions. He told them it was essential to confess their crimes if they were to find eternal rest and peace. When confronted, Bland denied striking Martha, but Bonsall, his guard down, exclaimed, 'Thou didst strike her Will'. This slip made it clear that Bonsall, who had continued to maintain his innocence since the trial ended, had been present at Stanley Hall, and he finally admitted that it was he who had struck the blows that killed Martha.

Further confessions followed, and it emerged that the three men had committed many crimes together, including highway robbery, dwelling house burglaries, and mill breaking. Bonsall told Revd Vevers that he had stolen the crowbar used to kill his victim from a blacksmith's forge in Matlock, with a different crime in view. He and an accomplice he refused to name had intended to rob and murder a woman who kept a tollgate between Matlock and Bakewell. When they arrived they saw their intended victim sitting alone by her fire. They were about to enter the house when a carriage approached, and they decided to abandon their plans.

Martha Goddard had not been so fortunate, but it is clear that with their executions a trio of murderous criminals had been removed from society.

2

A CUCKOLD'S
BLOODY REVENGE

Belper, 1844

On the morning of Monday, 22 April 1844, fifty-year-old William Yeomans, a millwright employed at Strutt's Mill in Belper, called at the Red Lion Hotel. He asked for a quart of gin, and complained to the landlady, 'I am dying fast, as I am landed with a bad woman'. The landlady knew him well as he was a regular customer, and in recent weeks she had often heard him complain about his wife, whom he would also sometimes threaten with violence. His complaint was therefore nothing new to the landlady, and in an attempt to calm him down she expressed the belief that everything would soon be all right between them.

However, on this occasion his words would prove to be no idle threat, for within hours Yeomans and his wife, Sarah, would suffer violent and bloody deaths. There would be no criminal trial, but at the inquest into the killings a story would emerge of betrayal, jealousy and despair, that would lead to murder and suicide.

The inquest into both deaths, at which the tragic tale was revealed, was held at the Red Lion Hotel on Wednesday, 24 April before the local coroner, Henry Mozley. The first witness to be called was Hannah Godbehere, who had known William and Sarah Yeomans all of her life, and had been their next-door neighbour for several years. She told the inquest that she had been aware that her neighbours' marriage had been unhappy for many months. The reason for this had been Sarah's more or less open intimate relationship with a twenty-year-old nailer and local man, George Ride.

Hannah described a conversation she had with William a few days before the tragedy, in which he complained bitterly that, despite it having

Belper was the location of a tragic murder and suicide. (Author's collection)

been necessary for him to enter Derby Infirmary six weeks earlier as an in-patient due to a serious heart problem, he had been unable to stay for as long as his doctor had wanted him to. This, he claimed, was due to his having discovered his wife's affair with Ride. He had discharged himself and was now attending the infirmary as an out-patient.

Hannah had also spoken to William on the Saturday before the killings, the day when matters had seemingly come to a head. William had told her that Sarah had offered to travel to Derby to collect her husband's medicine, which he had agreed to. However, as he waited for her to return he began to suspect that she would take the opportunity to meet her young lover. He therefore left the house and kept watch on the Derby road, awaiting her return. When he first saw her she was alone, but as she drew nearer to the village, Ride approached her, and William watched in horror as they embraced. He immediately confronted them, and punched Sarah to the ground, but before he could assault her lover, Ride ran away. William continued complaining to Hannah that his wife's relationship with George Ride had led to her spending a great deal of money and to her neglecting her own family and home. Furthermore, he admitted to Hannah that in revenge for his wife's scandalous behaviour, he had recently burnt some of her clothes.

The witness continued her evidence by stating that as she and Yeoman spoke, Sarah, who had left the house earlier that morning, returned. Hannah watched as William approached her in a threatening manner, and she could see that Sarah, who tried to step back, was terrified. William grabbed her by the throat and forced her indoors. A short time later, Hannah saw Sarah run from the house, to which she did not return until the following morning.

The next witness was Sarah Watson, who had also been a neighbour of the couple, and who was aware of the marital difficulties they were experiencing. Early on Saturday morning, Sarah Yeomans had visited her home, saying William had threatened to kill her and she was terrified that he might carry out his threat. As the two women spoke William arrived, demanding to speak to his wife. However, after seeing her husband approach, Sarah locked herself in an outhouse and refused to come out to speak to him. A furious William told his neighbour that he had tolerated his wife's adultery for too long and he was prepared to kill her and commit suicide afterwards.

However, William had left the scene without causing any difficulties, and later, Sarah was persuaded to return home by her friend, who had thought that he had simply been making empty threats. The next Sarah heard of the Yeomans was on the following Monday, when Hannah Godbehere ran to her house to tell her of terrible screams that had been heard coming from their home.

The next witness was Jane Godbehere, Hannah's daughter, who described the events she had witnessed on the day of the tragedy. At 1.40 p.m. she heard what she recognised as blows being struck next door, which were followed by a piercing scream, which she knew immediately was coming from Sarah as she had heard her being beaten on several occasions in the past. She alerted her mother who went to find help, but meanwhile Jane heard Sarah scream a few times more until they eventually came to an end. There was silence for some minutes, before Jane ventured out to join her mother and other neighbours, who had approached the house and were attempting to force the front door open.

The chronicle of events was continued by Samuel Allen, a thirteen-year-old boy who travelled around the Derbyshire countryside selling ribbons, tapes and pins. On the day of the tragedy, he came to Belper and decided to call on Sarah Yeomans, who in the past had been a good customer. However, instead of selling some of his wares, he was to become the only eyewitness to the events that occurred in the Yeomans' house, and he described them to a hushed coroner's court.

When he reached the house Samuel knocked on the door, but there was no reply. He knocked for a second time, and as he did so he heard a loud scream coming from inside. He rushed to a window, through which he saw William and Sarah standing about 4ft apart and facing each other. They were standing very close to the window, but both seemed unaware of Samuel's presence.

William, who was holding a poker, was described by the lad as being in a great rage, and Sarah looked terrified. Samuel watched helplessly as William struck his wife a severe blow to the head with the poker, forcing her to the floor. He then stood over the desperate woman and struck her several more blows. She continued to scream out, but after a few moments she fell silent.

Then, Samuel saw William take a chair from next to the fireplace and place it in the centre of the room, close to where Sarah lay. He sat in the chair with his back towards Samuel, who saw him take a knife from his pocket, which he opened, thus exposing the blade. In one smooth movement, William put the blade to a point just under his left ear and proceeded to slit his own throat. Although William had his back to him, Samuel saw a huge amount of blood spurt from the wound, and watched as he fell from the chair to the floor. Moments later, the group of neighbours broke down the front door and rushed into the room.

William Sims, the village blacksmith, had known William and Sarah for more than twenty years, and was a close neighbour. In describing William, he told the coroner's jury that, until recently, he had never known a more placid individual. However, after he had learnt of his wife's adulterous affair, his behaviour had changed dramatically, and whenever he met him he seemed to be always agitated and angry.

The witness had heard William threaten to kill his wife and himself if she did not end the affair. So worried was the blacksmith, that he had shared his concerns with the Yeomans' eldest son, and suggested that he keep an eye on his father to try and ensure he did nothing foolish.

Mr Sims also told the court that he was the first to arrive at the scene after the alarm had been raised, and it was he who broke the front door down. However, once inside the house, the witness became so distressed at what he saw that he had to leave almost immediately.

That Sarah's murder and William's suicide were premeditated acts became clear from the evidence given by Francis Garrett, a local joiner, who had also known William for a number of years. At 7.15 a.m. on the day of the deaths, after leaving the Red Lion Hotel, William visited the witness's shop. He produced a pocket knife, which was the one he used to kill himself with later that day. He asked Francis if he could sharpen it on an oilstone in the joiner's shop, saying he wanted it to cut his corns. The witness noticed nothing unusual about his visitor's demeanour, but he did leave the shop immediately he had completed his task, rather than stop and talk as he usually did.

Graphic medical evidence was provided by Dr Thomas Lomas, who had been called to the scene within minutes of the killings. He found William lying on his back in a position consistent with Samuel Allen's evidence. His throat was cut from about 2in below the left ear almost

The home of William and Sarah Yeomans, in which they met violent deaths. (The Derby & Chesterfield Reporter and Derbyshire Chronicle)

across to the right ear. The wound was 7in long, and the vertebrae of the neck were exposed. The pocket knife, which had caused the fatal wound and which was covered in the deceased's blood, lay close to the man's body. Although not dead when the doctor arrived, William expired within a very short time.

Sarah was lying on her front, with her hands positioned as though she had been attempting to protect her head. There were three fractures to her skull, and she had received several other serious head wounds. The poker lay close to her body and was covered in her blood and hair. Her ring finger was broken; an injury sustained as she had attempted to defend herself. Sarah was alive and she remained conscious until she died twenty-four hours later. A post-mortem confirmed that death was due to serious head injuries.

Despite not having been called as a witness to give formal evidence at the inquest, the coroner summoned George Ride, a central figure in the tragedy. This had been at the request of the jury, as its members wished him to receive some form of reprimand from the coroner. This was due to what the jury had described as his 'immoral and profligate conduct'. The coroner needed no persuading, and made it clear to the young man that he believed his reprehensible behaviour had been the most significant contributory factor to the deaths that were being enquired into.

The coroner next addressed the jury, pointing out that there could be no question as to who was actually responsible for the killings. The only issue to be determined was the state of mind of William Yeomans at the time.

As far as the coroner was concerned there had been no evidence presented to suggest that he had been insane.

The jury retired, and on their return they advised the coroner that they disagreed with him, as it was their unanimous belief that William was insane when he killed his wife and himself. The coroner adjourned the inquest until the following day when the issue of William's sanity would be addressed more fully.

At the resumed hearing, Hannah Yeomans, the ten-year-old daughter of the deceased couple, was the first to be called to give evidence. Although it must have been extremely distressing for her, she spoke in a clear and firm voice. She told the court that in the recent past she had come to realise that her parents were unhappy, and despite her young age, she was aware that this stemmed from her mother's relationship with George Ride. Hannah worked at Strutt's Mill, and when she left for work at 6 a.m. on the morning of the killings, her father was pacing up and down the street outside their house, and as she passed him he nodded to her but did not speak.

Hannah did not go home for breakfast, as her mother delivered it to her at work two hours later. However, she arrived home at a few minutes after twelve o'clock for lunch, which was eaten in silence, with her parents and her sister and brother. This was until her mother said she was going into the yard for some water. However, her father would not let her do so as he said that George Ride would be outside, and he told Hannah to go to the pump instead. Hannah could see that all was not well, but she noticed no significant difference in her father's behaviour, and he appeared quiet and calm.

John Yeomans, the disabled son of the deceased couple, was the next witness to be called to give evidence. He was unable to work and had lived with his parents all of his life. On the day of the killings he recalled his mother leaving the house to take Hannah her breakfast at the mill. As she left the house he heard his father shout to her, and, pointing to what he described as his wasting body, told her that he was so weak he would not be able to work for much longer due to his failing health.

His father had then produced two phials, and told John that he would visit the chemist to obtain a large enough quantity of laudanum to fill both of them. He returned home at half past ten without the drug, as the chemist had none in store. A few minutes later John's sister-in-law called at the house to ask the young man to look after her child while she saw to some household chores. As he picked up his crutches, his father grabbed him, saying he should not go until after dinner, which John felt was most unusual, and he also noticed that his father was sweating profusely. As far as John was concerned his father was not of sound mind, and had not been so for the previous three months.

A neighbour, Alexander Sanders, told the court that he had met William at about eleven o'clock on the morning of the killings. William complained that a few minutes earlier, George Ride and a companion had passed by his house, and seeing William, they had both shouted abuse and ridiculed him. William told Sanders that he felt disturbed in the mind and did not know what to do. He had considered travelling to see his brother in Nottingham but was too ill to make the journey. William muttered to himself a great deal, and the witness felt that he was of unsound mind at that time.

Next on the stand was wood turner Charles Seal, who was chairman of the Druid's Club, to which members made weekly contributions, thus entitling them to claim financial benefits when unable to work. William had continued to work after leaving hospital, but he had to work fewer hours and could only perform light duties. This meant that he was not receiving his full wage, which the club was supplementing. Mr Seal had called to see William a few days before the killings to pay him his sickness benefit. As he collected it, William told his visitor that he had heard a rumour that his benefit payments were soon to be stopped as he was rumoured to have been beating his wife, although he insisted he had only hit her once with an umbrella. The chairman tried to reassure him that this was not so, and he would continue to receive his payments from the club.

Mr Seal continued by advising the coroner and the jury that he had considered William to have been of unsound mind for at least six weeks. He had accompanied him to consult Dr Lomas, who had confirmed that William was suffering from a serious heart complaint, and that he must therefore avoid heavy work, and must not become excited in any way. This was because it would take very little for his heart to stop. This news had clearly alarmed William, who afterwards seemed much disturbed.

The last witness to be called was William Williamson, a longstanding friend of the deceased couple, who explained that he had been very concerned at the difficulties he knew they had been experiencing. He called on them at 12.45 p.m. on the fateful day and was the last person to see them alive and to talk with them. He stayed with them for approximately twenty minutes, in the hope that there was something he could do to help. During the period he stayed with them, William had seemed restless, and continuously paced about the room.

On one occasion the pacing stopped abruptly and he lay down on the sofa. Sarah approached him, but before she could speak, her husband waved her away, saying, 'I'll hear no more of it. I am at peace with you, and I will be'. He rose to his feet, and, grabbing hold of his thigh, said, 'I'm wasted to nothing, I must soon be gone'. He next put his hand to his stomach and said he felt ill. Mr Williamson left, and as he did so, William said to him, 'I'll never be any better'. Thirty minutes later William was dead and Sarah had been fatally wounded.

This was the conclusion of the additional evidence called by the coroner to establish William's state of mind at the time he killed his wife and himself. The jury again retired and after only a short time, they returned with their decision. As far as they were concerned that morning's evidence supported the conclusion they had reached the previous day. They believed that William had killed his wife and himself while labouring under a fit of temporary insanity. On hearing the decision the coroner repeated that he did not agree with their findings, for as far as he was concerned no proof of his insanity had been provided.

Whatever the truth of the matter, it is clear that for some weeks William had known of his wife's affair with George Ride, and this was the cause of much emotional turmoil. His physical health was deteriorating and he seemed convinced that he was about to die. On the day of the killings he had been taunted by Ride, which must have been especially distressing.

Who was right about William's state of mind – the coroner or the jury – is something of a moot point. The simple fact is that a jealous and vengeful man, feeling a great sense of betrayal, had decided that no other man would have his wife.

3

THE BODY IN THE CESSPIT

Chesterfield, 1845

The cesspit in the yard of Chesterfield flour dealer George Bunting was 5ft deep and 8ft wide, and served his house and that of his neighbours, Mr and Mrs Townsend. It was now full, and Mr Bunting hired three men to empty it and spread its contents on his field, which was located close by.

On 28 August 1846 he employed Valentine Wall and Richard Ashley, who had the task of emptying the pit of its contents, and Thomas Green, who was responsible for spreading the manure on the field. After removing thirty or so buckets, Valentine and Richard noticed a number of bones, which they at first presumed to be those of an animal. However, within a few minutes they found several items of men's clothing, which included remnants of a coat, a pair of trousers and a hat. They very soon recovered several more bones which were clearly human, namely two thigh bones and an arm bone, from which, to their horror, some remaining flesh fell off when they picked it up. Meanwhile, Thomas also noticed some men's clothing in the field, and salvaged some stockings, braces and a neckerchief. He also came across some ribs and leg bones, and attached to the latter were two garters, one white and the other red.

When told of the discoveries, Mr Bunting consulted two of his friends, butcher Mr Wyatt and Dr Hugh Walker. It was confirmed that these were indeed human bones, and a further search revealed many more, including a skull. The police were advised and after an extensive search throughout the day, an almost complete human skeleton was found in the cesspit, with only a few small bones and teeth missing. Dr Walker confirmed it was the skeleton of a man.

He found three fractures to the skull, one of which was a little above the right eye, and another close to the left eye; all of the small bones around the eyes had been shattered. The other was at the base of the skull, and all three had been caused by violent blows with a blunt instrument, similar to the stave which was 3ft long and which had also been found in the cesspit. At this stage an accidental death or suicide could not be ruled out completely, but it was obviously a suspicious death of some kind.

Mr Bunting had hired Thomas Cowley to empty the cesspit fourteen months earlier, and Thomas told police that he had emptied it completely. He had seen no bones or clothes, and was adamant that he would have noticed if there had been any present at that time. Therefore, the police were convinced that the body had found its way into the pit within the previous fourteen months, which led them to recall the mysterious disappearance of twenty-six-year-old George Collis on Sunday, 7 December 1845.

Officers visited George's mother, Mary Mawkes, and his girlfriend, Ellen Berresford, both of whom had seen him on the day of his disappearance. Both confirmed that the items of clothing found in the pit were those that George had been wearing that day. In particular, Ellen clearly remembered that he had been wearing one red and one white garter. She was also able to identify the neckerchief as she had hemmed it for him.

Ellen and George's mother had reported his disappearance at the time, but the absence of a body, and there being no evidence of his having been the victim of foul play, meant that the police had been unable to initiate a meaningful investigation. However, they now had grounds to look into the circumstances surrounding his disappearance, and were able to commit the necessary resources to the case.

The police were aware that George had arranged to meet John Platts on the evening of 7 December 1845. The two men had recently become partners in a small butchering business. George contributed the necessary finances and business expertise, and his partner, who had worked as a butcher in the past, provided the necessary practical expertise.

Joseph Heathcote told the police that he had seen George leaving Ellen Berresford's house at about 6.30 p.m. on the night of his disappearance. Later, he saw George and Platts in the shop of a man named Morley in the Shambles district, and as the door was open he could see the partners apparently having an argument. Platts was holding an axe, which at one point he banged against a block of wood as though to emphasise a point. Joseph continued walking, and after taking several more steps he heard the sound of something falling. As it seemed to come from the shop, he turned to investigate, but the door slammed shut and he could see nothing more.

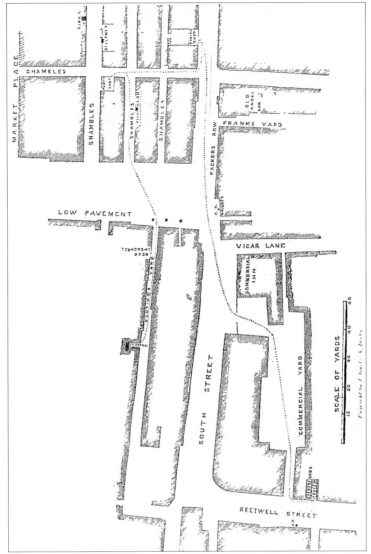

A contemporary plan of the Shambles. The dotted line from the Berresford house to Morley's shop, is the route taken by Collis when he was seen by John Heathcote. The witness went round by South Street, and when he passed Morley's shop, Collis was there. The dotted line from there to Platts' shop is the route taken by Morley and Platts when supporting Collis in an apparently drunken state. The other dotted line leads from here to the cesspit. (The Derby & Chesterfield Reporter and Derbyshire Chronicle)

Thirty minutes later, Samuel Slack of Brampton, who was visiting his sister in the Shambles district, saw three men leaving Morley's premises. Two of them were apparently holding up a drunken companion between them, who was incapable of supporting himself. Samuel watched as the trio reached Platts' shop, and saw the two men push their drunken acquaintance head first into the premises. He heard the sound of the door being locked from inside, and saw the curtains pulled shut.

A few minutes later, a group of six people who were celebrating a wedding and visiting the public houses in the Shambles, passed Platts' shop; they were Thomas and Elizabeth Harvey, Thomas and Phoebe Bellamy, together with James Kirk and his sister-in-law, Ann Kirk. The group heard moans coming from inside the shop, followed by the sound of something apparently being dragged along the floor. Elizabeth shouted through the locked door, asking if everything was all right. Platts did not open the door but shouted back that he was alone and had been sick.

Those in the wedding party were aware that Platts had been courting a local young woman named Hannah, and initially they were worried that he might be beating her. Accordingly, Ann Kirk went to Hannah's house which was nearby, to confirm that she was well, and the party moved on to the next public house, having satisfied themselves that Hannah was unharmed.

Later, at about 9.30 p.m., Platts entered Thomas Bellamy's public house, which was opposite his shop. Several customers noticed that he had a freshly cut hand, which he explained was due to his having caught it on a hook in his shop. Mrs Bellamy offered to dress it for him, and as she did so, Thomas Harvey shouted over to him, 'Jack, I could have sworn you had somebody in that shop'. Ann Kirk told Platts that she had called at Hannah's home to ensure that she was well. His injured hand having been tended to, an annoyed Platts left but returned a few minutes later with Hannah, to prove to the other customers in the pub that she was well and had not been assaulted by him.

Later that night Platts called in at the Old Angel, which he usually visited each Sunday to spend time with the church bell-ringers after the final service of the day. The landlady, Catherine Frank, noticed his injured hand, and when asked about it he gave the same explanation he had given earlier. He also told her that he had decided to visit Mansfield to enter a raffle for a watch, which would prove to be highly significant in later months when the investigation into the murder of George Collis was underway.

The police heard further interesting information from John Heathcote. On the night of Monday, 8 December, he had arranged to meet his brother, Godfrey, at the Peacock Inn in the Shambles. At ten o'clock, the two brothers saw Platts, Morley and a third man they did not recognise, carrying a heavy sack. They were making their way from Platts' shop, and the Heathcotes presumed the sack was full of offal, which the three men were going to dispose of. The three men stopped several times to rest, suggesting that the contents of the sack were heavy. They eventually reached the entrance to Bunting's yard, which they turned into.

After a few days, a number of people approached Platts to enquire about his business partner's whereabouts. Thomas Harvey actually told friends that he believed Platts had murdered George, and he approached Platts demanding to know what had happened to him. He was told that George had travelled to either Macclesfield or Manchester. Others were also suspicious and in June 1846, Platts was haymaking with Humphrey Belfit, who also asked after George. Platts assured him that he had seen him six weeks earlier in Manchester. When Humphrey persisted in asking more questions, Platts refused to discuss the matter further.

Following the discovery of the remains in Mr Bunting's cesspit, and before they had been identified as being those of Collis, Platts was asked by a friend, Caroline Radmill, what he thought had happened to his former partner. In reply, Platts suggested that he might have killed himself, and explained that a few days before George's disappearance he had come across the deceased, who was alone and holding a razor to his throat. Platts alleged that George told him he had been contemplating suicide for some time.

Of the three men seen carrying the heavy sack into Mr Bunting's yard on the night that George Collis disappeared, one remained unidentified, and another, Morley, had since died of typhus. The police believed they had gathered sufficient information to focus their attention on John Platts, and on 3 September he was interviewed by Inspector Charles Cotterill. Platts insisted that he had not been involved in the killing of George Collis, and stated that he had last seen him on Saturday, 6 December at Platts' market stall. George had asked if he could borrow £2 10s, to which Platts agreed. Platts denied owing money to his partner, and insisted that George owed him £9. The two of them had arranged to meet on the following day, but George had not kept the appointment. As for his own movements on the day of the disappearance, Platts told the inspector that he had been in the Old Angel public house between the hours of six and eleven that night.

This did not satisfy the police, and on the following day a search was made of the suspect's house. A watch was found together with a pair of boots, which the police were convinced belonged to the dead man. Platts advised them that he had bought the watch off William Beaumont, who was also known as 'Lanky Bill', a local criminal who lived with two prostitutes. When questioned by the police later, Beaumont denied having ever possessed the watch, and a Chesterfield watchmaker,

John Thompson, identified it as one he had sold to George Collis on 29 December 1839. The boots were also found to have belonged to George Collis, for whom a local cobbler, Mr Shore, confirmed he had made them.

To add to his problems, the landlord and landlady of the Old Angel did not support Platt's alibi. This, when viewed with his inability to explain how the watch and boots came to be in his possession, led to Platts being arrested and charged with murder. His trial took place at the Derby Assizes on Friday, 19 March 1847 before Mr Justice Patterson, in a packed courtroom. The prosecution was led by Mr Humphrey QC, assisted by Mr Mellor, and the accused was represented by Mr McCauley and Mr W.H. Adams.

There were no witnesses to the crime, and no murder weapon had been identified, but the prosecution believed that they had a strong case and would be able to persuade the jury of the prisoner's guilt. They called as witnesses those who had been present at the events of the relevant Sunday and Monday nights. The prosecution cast doubt on Platts' alibi for the night of the disappearance; Lanky Bill was called to testify that the watch had never been in his possession, and proof that the boots had been made for the deceased was provided. The prosecution advised the jury that it was not necessary to provide a motive for the crime, but it was believed that the accused owed the dead man money, which he had simply decided not to repay, and to avoid doing so he had opted to murder George.

The prosecution's case was that the victim was either killed or incapacitated in Morley's shop, before being taken to Platts' premises, where, if not already dead, he was murdered and his body dismembered. On the following night the body parts were placed in a sack and taken to the cesspit, into which it was thrown by the accused and his two fellow conspirators. Mr Humphrey claimed that the combined testimonies of the witnesses proved that Platts was one of the three men involved in this dreadful crime.

The defence relied on attempting to discredit the prosecution witnesses, and on character witnesses which they called to testify on their client's behalf. John and Godfrey Healthcare were accused of making up their respective testimonies from newspaper accounts; Catherine Franks who testified that the accused had not spent the whole night of the murder in the Old Angel, was described as having confused that night with another; the defence claimed it was too dark for Samuel Slack to have seen the events he described; and Thomas Harvey was accused of being drunk on the night in question and was thus an unreliable witness. It was Lanky Bill, however, who came in for the most scathing criticism. He had served several prison sentences, and

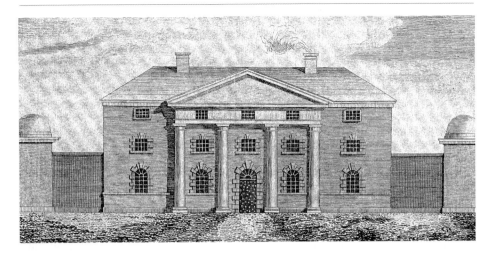

Platts was hanged outside Derby Gaol. (Derby Local Studies Library)

Mr McCauley suggested that he was in fact one of the murderers and was attempting to lay the blame on an innocent man so that he might escape justice.

Mr McCauley next called two character witnesses. The first was Robert Statham, a butcher who had employed the accused for several years, and Revd Holden, both of whom described a mild-mannered and honest young man, whom they believed incapable of committing such a crime. In his final address to the jury, Mr McCauley claimed that there was no real proof that George Collis was dead or that the body in the cesspit was his. Furthermore, there was no conclusive proof that the sack being carried by the three men contained a body. Nor, he contended, had the Crown produced any evidence that his client owed George Collis any money.

In his summing up, the judge highlighted the absence of any direct evidence linking the accused to the murder, and it would be for the jury to decide whether or not he was implicated in any crime. The jury members remained in their seats and, having conferred for two minutes, returned a guilty verdict. Sentencing him to death, the judge warned Platts not to expect a reprieve.

In his final days, Platts wrote two letters, one to his mother and the other to Mr Statham, thanking him for his support at the trial. He also left a written confession in which he attempted to minimise his own involvement in the crime. He acknowledged that he did participate, and implicated Morley and the other unnamed man. It was they, he claimed, who planned the crime, and he insisted that he did not personally strike the victim, nor did he assist in the dismemberment of the body.

Platts was hanged at noon on Thursday, 1 April 1847, outside the walls of Derby Gaol. There were several thousand spectators, many of whom had travelled from Chesterfield by special excursion trains. The condemned man spent much of the morning in the chapel, until, at 11.50 a.m., the bell tolled, signifying the execution was to take place. He made his way to the gallows with a firm step, but when he stepped on to the drop his legs began to shake violently. The drop opened and after struggling for two minutes, Platts was pronounced dead. After the formalities of the inquest on his body had been completed, he was, in accordance with tradition, buried within the gaol's walls.

4

MURDERED FOR
AN INHERITANCE

Ilkeston, 1861

It was the spring of 1861, and Joseph Smith, a forty-six-year-old successful shoemaker, was living on Bath Street, Ilkeston, in one of a row of four cottages, all of which he owned. Joseph shared his home with his three sons, thirteen-year-old Edwin, sixteen-year-old Henry, and George, who was twenty. Henry and his father shared one bedroom, and George and Edwin shared another. Edwin was still attending school, Henry worked alongside his father in the family business, and George was employed as a lace maker with Messrs Ball & Co. of Ilkeston. Joseph's married daughter, Sarah, lived next door with her husband Aaron Aldred.

George was a feckless individual, with a reputation for womanising and irresponsible behaviour. Two women were reportedly pregnant by him at the time, and he planned to marry one of them, Ellen Cox, at Whitsuntide. This was against the wishes of his father, and this opposition to his relationship with his fiancée was placing additional stress on the already strained relationship between father and son.

Joseph had been widowed for seven years, and although he had remarried in 1859, he and his second wife had separated. Following his first wife's death he had suffered periods of depression and had turned to alcohol to alleviate the pain of his loss. On more than one occasion he had appeared in front of his children holding an open razor, threatening to kill himself and the whole family. However, it had been more than a year since such an incident had occurred.

Monday, 1 May began like most other days. The family ate breakfast together, after which Joseph and Henry left for work, at seven o'clock. However, George had arranged to change shifts with a friend, Reuben

Davis, and would not be going to work. Unbeknown to his father, George had taken Joseph's bank-book, and had decided to travel to Nottingham where his father had an account containing £144 with the Nottingham Savings Bank, to withdraw some of the money.

As he walked to the station, George met a friend, Henry Davis, and asked if he wanted to travel to Nottingham with him. Henry had no money, but agreed to go when George said he would pay his fare, and the pair took the eleven o'clock train. In the days that followed, the police were able to trace George's movements that day from a number of witnesses.

Henry told them that on arrival in Nottingham, George went to the bank, where John Stevenson dealt with him. George produced his father's bank-book and asked to withdraw £14. However, he was told that it would not be possible, as before he could withdraw any cash he would need to produce a letter signed by his father allowing him to do so.

Henry had not realised that George had his father's bank-book until he met him later at the wine and spirits vault owned by John Bridger, who knew Joseph Smith. George agreed a loan of £1 with John, after offering to leave the bank-book as security and promising to return the following day to repay the loan.

At midday, George and Henry walked to the Tom Moody public house, where George met prostitute Elizabeth Meakin, who had known him for ten months. She told the police that she sat with the two men for fifteen minutes before George said he was going to visit a nearby shop. He left them three pence with which to purchase drinks, and returned some time later. He showed them a pocketbook and a pair of boots he had just purchased, but it was his other purchases which would later interest the police.

George had visited David Webster's pawn shop on Clumber Street, where, after examining several weapons, he bought a pistol costing 4s. As Mr Webster did not sell powder and shot, he directed George to the shop of Eliza Carr, which was directly opposite his own. Later, when questioned by the police, she would have no difficulty remembering him, in view of his antics in her shop. He bought a halfpenny worth of caps, took out his pistol and placed one in it, telling the shopkeeper, 'I want it to fit very well'. He was about to pull the trigger, but Mrs Carr prevented him from firing it in the shop, so he went outside and did so. Before leaving he paid one penny for a small amount of powder.

Having returned to the Tom Moody pub, it was agreed that Henry should wait there while George went with Elizabeth to her house in Bell Yard. There, he showed her the pistol, but said he did not want Henry to know he had bought it. She asked George why he wanted the weapon, to which he replied, 'I want to shoot with it at night.' When she told him, 'You may do some harm with that', he replied, 'I shall do no one no harm that does me none, but I would shoot my own father if he was to offend me.' They returned to the Tom Moody and after a few more drinks, George and Henry took the evening train to Ilkeston, where they arrived at 7.30 p.m.

George and Henry parted at the railway station, but a few minutes later George met his friend's brother, Reuben Davis. Reuben asked George to lend him sixpence so that he could buy some shot and powder from Mr Chadwick's shop, as he wished to shoot some wood pigeons. George agreed to do so, and also gave him six caps. It was now eight o'clock, and George decided to go home for some bread and cheese, but the two young men arranged to meet later at the Queen's Head public house.

However, it would emerge later that before going to meet Reuben, George approached an eight-year-old girl, Martha Cockayne, and asked her to purchase one pennyworth of shot from Isaac Gregory's shop, and this was later confirmed by the shopkeeper when he was visited by the police.

George met Reuben as they had arranged, but left at ten o'clock, saying he would return soon. When he did so, he told Reuben, 'As soon as I got home, my father ran into the pantry'. Reuben asked why he should have done such a thing, to which George replied, 'I don't know why, but I believe my father will make away with himself before long, he seems so uneasy.' They parted company at a few minutes to midnight.

Earlier that evening Joseph and Henry had finished work, and the older man visited his brother Samuel, at whose house he arrived at nine o'clock. Samuel later advised the police that his brother stayed for about thirty minutes and had appeared to be in good spirits.

Henry visited the home of a friend, Edwin Dakin, where he stayed for two hours. He arrived home at 10.15 p.m. to find his father still dressed and lying on the sofa. Edwin arrived home a few minutes later. Henry asked if George had been home, to which his father replied that he had called at the house briefly before going out again. The two boys and their father ate a supper of bread and milk together, after which Joseph told his sons to go to bed. This was at 11.40 p.m. and both boys later told the police that their father seemed well and that he had not been drinking. Joseph told his sons that he would smoke his pipe for a few minutes before going to bed. A short time later, he climbed into bed next to Henry, but ten minutes later he got out and went downstairs. A few minutes later, Henry heard George enter the house.

Henry heard his father and brother begin to argue almost immediately, and he heard his father shout 'George, you see what trouble you have brought yourself into. I shall not leave my door undone for you any longer, and if you cannot keep proper hours you will have to go somewhere else.' George made no reply, and Joseph told him to go to bed. However, this was followed by what Henry recognised to be a gunshot.

Bath Street, Ilkeston. (Author's collection)

Henry was joined in his room by Edwin, who had also heard the shot, and the two terrified boys went to the bedroom window, which they opened. The boys seemed to have realised instinctively what had occurred and, being frightened that George might decide to kill them next, they screamed for help. Their cries of 'Murder! Murder!' were heard by their sister next door.

She hurried outside to be told by the boys, who were leaning out of the window, 'George has killed our father, do come!' She rushed into the house alone, where she found her father's body, but there was no sign of George. Although overcome with horror, she still had the presence of mind to check for signs of life. However, there were none and she went for her husband, Aaron, but he was already on his way, having heard his wife's screams. Aaron's brother Isaac, who also lived on the row of houses on Bath Street, had also heard the shot and screams. He ran to the house and, with his brother, made sure that Henry and Edwin were safe.

A few minutes later George walked into the house accompanied by Reuben Davis. Isaac shouted, 'What have you done George? You have killed your father!' George replied by saying, 'No, no, no, he's done it himself'. He was then asked 'Where's the pistol if he did it himself?' George explained 'I took it and hurled it away'. At this point Isaac believed that George was about to run off so he grabbed him to prevent him from doing so, exclaiming, 'You villain, you have shot your father!'

Sarah and Aaron also accused George of Joseph's murder, but he persisted in claiming his innocence, saying, 'Aaron I am innocent. Will you believe me? Shake hands with me'.

Constables George Carling and Charles Ridge were on their beat on Bath Street, and heard the shouted accusations of murder. They entered the house and heard Henry once more accuse George of shooting his father. George denied it yet again and tried to embrace his younger brother, who pulled away in revulsion. George then threw himself dramatically across the body of his father, and kissed him. Constable Carling pulled him off, and on the basis of the accusations made by those in the house, immediately arrested him, saying, 'I take you on a charge of shooting your father.'

George, who knew the officer, became hysterical and screamed, 'Give me my father's big knife. I will have my revenge. I will plunge it through Carling's heart!' Ignoring this threat to his life, the police officer held on to his prisoner, while his colleague went for Superintendent Hudson. On his arrival, the superintendent ordered that George be taken to the lock-up.

The superintendent next sent for Dr George Norman, who on his arrival found Joseph's body surrounded by a great deal of blood, in which he noticed several fragments of brain. There was a massive gaping wound to the left side of the head, from which a large portion of brain was protruding. The doctor concluded that the weapon used must have been held close to the head at the time the trigger was pulled. Following his initial examination, Dr Norman placed the blood and pieces of brain from the floor into a bucket, which he took away for further examination.

Later, the doctor performed a post-mortem, and on closer examination of the head wound, he noted that the entry point was located above and a little behind the left ear. He placed his finger into the head and discovered several bone fragments had been driven into the brain. He further discovered that the shot had passed through the middle lobe of the brain, in a downward direction. Between thirty and forty pieces of shot were removed from the head and brain during the post-mortem.

Coincidentally, the deceased had been a patient of Dr Norman's, who was therefore aware that Joseph had been right handed. The doctor concluded that the wound that had killed Joseph could not have been caused by his own hand, and therefore the possibility of suicide was eliminated. The most plausible scenario was that whoever had killed Joseph had shot him from behind, and had been standing slightly higher than the victim. Furthermore, the killer, who must have been standing very close to the deceased, would, he believed, have blood on his hand and lower arm and also on the sleeve of any garment being worn at the time of the shooting.

Nevertheless, in a statement he made to the police following his arrest, George persisted with his claim that his father had shot himself. He described his father sitting to one side of the fireplace, and he on the other. His father had reportedly told him, 'George, you are killing me by inches', and without any warning, he had produced the pistol and shot himself before George could do anything to prevent him from doing so.

George's statement continued by suggesting that his father had been threatening to kill himself for some considerable time. In support of this he mentioned a letter he had written recently to his fiancée stating that he believed his father would commit suicide in the near future. However, the police were convinced that this had been part of George's plan to persuade people that his father was suicidal, in an attempt to divert suspicion from himself and disguise the fact that a murder was going to take place. The police had learnt from other family members that despite Joseph's past threats to kill himself, none had been made for more than a year.

The inquest into Joseph's death opened before the coroner, Mr W. Whiston at the Queen's Head on the afternoon of 3 May. Following formal identification of the body, details of the post-mortem were provided by Dr Norman and the events surrounding the death were described by the Smith family. The police were granted their wish for an adjournment until the following week so that they could continue with their enquiries.

In the days that followed, Joseph's bank-book was retrieved from Nottingham and Constable Jesse Burdening conducted a search for the murder weapon. He found the pistol 100 yards from the Smith home. The police traced Ann Eyre, one of George's former lovers, who remembered him saying that he wished his father would die so that he might inherit his fortune. It was common knowledge that Joseph had not made a will as he always stated that he had no intention of dying in the near future. Lace maker Elijah Ellis, who worked alongside George, told of a conversation he had with him a few days before the crime. George had asked Elijah if being the eldest son meant that his father's money and property would automatically come to him in the absence of a will, should Joseph die. The police interviewed George Kerry, a friend of George's fiancée Ellen Cox, who lived in Belton, Leicestershire. He stated that a few days before the shooting he had heard George say to Ellen that they would be able to marry in the near future as 'I expect to receive my fortune next week'. All of this information persuaded the police that they had a motive for the murder, as they were convinced that George had committed the premeditated crime in order to inherit his father's fortune.

Blood was found on the sleeve of the shirt George was wearing at the time the shooting took place, but unfortunately for the investigators, no witness could be found who could state definitely that they had seen it on his clothing before he threw himself on his father's body. This could not therefore be used as evidence against him.

Two new witnesses came forward who provided the police with further important information. Sophia Meakin and her niece Harriet Robinson had been walking close to the Smith house at the time of the shooting. Each of them was carrying a candle, which enabled them to recognise George as he entered his father's house. Almost immediately this was followed by a shot, and fearing for their safety they rushed home, but contacted the police on the following day, having heard of Joseph's death.

The death of their father and arrest of their brother had been a massive tragedy for the young Smith boys. The strain on Henry became evident at the inquest, where after more than an hour of questioning, he was asked by the coroner if he had ever previously seen the pistol that had been used to kill his father. Henry became distraught and began sobbing. He shouted at the coroner, 'I have never seen the pistol yet and I don't want to. You want to break my heart if you can!'

Eventually the testimonies of all the witnesses came to an end and the jury was asked to consider their verdict. They took two minutes to return a verdict of wilful murder against George, who was committed to stand trial at the next Derby Assizes. However, there still remained the need for another hearing before the local magistrates, within a few days of the inquest, at which all of the witnesses, including Henry, had to repeat their evidence in its entirety. With the trial at the assizes due to take place within a few weeks, this would mean Henry having to give evidence that could hang his brother on three occasions in public, and this was quite apart from the questioning by the police in private. This had long been a concern to many, and a correspondent wrote a letter to the *Derby Mercury*, who concluded his letter with the following sentiments:

The office of coroner is of very ancient origin, equal indeed in antiquity to the office of sheriff, and dates back as far as the Statute 3 Edward 1st; the authority of the magistrates going back to the Statute 34 Edward 3rd. It is true that in an examination before the magistrates the suspected person is compulsively present, but he may generally be present at a coroner's inquest. At any rate, the inquest is a transaction of public notoriety, and a prisoner is entitled to a copy of the depositions. I repeat therefore, in such a case as the present what practical good will result from the exercise of the concurrent jurisdiction of the magistrates? It will involve a great sacrifice of time, a large and useless expenditure of money in bringing the witnesses here, perhaps for two or three days, and entails on them the process of mental torture which common humanity suggests should be avoided. Mark the observation of the witness Henry Smith in reply to the searching but necessary examination of the coroner. Ought such scenes to be repeated without necessity?

Yours faithfully

INQUIRER
Derby May 9

Now that the inquest had been concluded, it was possible to arrange Joseph's funeral, which took place at the local parish church on the following Sunday. It was attended by a large number of mourners, as he was a well-known and respected member of the local community. He had also been an active member of the Manchester Order of Oddfellows, 100 of whom were present at the service.

George's trial took place at the Derby Summer Assizes, in late July, before Mr Justice Willes. The prosecutors were Mr Boden, Mr Huish and Mr Cave. The accused was represented by Mr O'Brien and Mr Stephen, and when arraigned, George pleaded not guilty to the murder of his father. The prosecution relied on those witnesses who had testified at the inquest and before the Ilkeston magistrates, claiming that the premeditated crime had been committed so that George could inherit his father's fortune, and that over a period of time beforehand the accused had deliberately set out to convince people that his father had been suicidal and would kill himself in the near future.

The defence called no witnesses, and simply suggested to the jury that all of the evidence was circumstantial. They emphasised the fact that in attempting to withdraw the money from his father's bank account in Nottingham, George had done nothing illegal. They also raised the history of suicide threats made by Joseph, several of which had been witnessed by other family members. This, it was suggested, meant that their client's claim that his father had shot himself could not be discounted. True, it might have been difficult for a right-handed man to cause the head wound that had killed him, but the prosecution had failed to produce any witness who had seen George fire the fatal shot. There was thus sufficient room for doubt that would enable the jury to return a verdict of not guilty.

Nevertheless, following a brief retirement, the jury returned with a verdict of guilty, and the judge prepared to sentence the prisoner to death. As he did so, in line with tradition, he asked George if he wished to say anything before sentence was passed. Usually there was a simple shake of the head or a murmured declaration of innocence from the dock. However, George subjected the court to a tirade which lasted for several minutes.

George Smith. (The Derby Telegraph)

Jumping on his chair in the dock, he proclaimed his innocence to those in the courtroom, and claimed that all of the prosecution witnesses had lied. He beat his chest with a clenched fist shouting, 'I am innocent, and I stand here with a clear conscience and an upright heart and contented mind. It is not likely that my hand is stained with my father's blood. No, I loved him and would not shed his blood!' Eventually he calmed down and resumed his seat.

An enraged Judge Willes sentenced the prisoner to death, and told him that the jury had reached the only verdict that was possible based on the evidence they had heard. Furthermore, his crime was so heinous he should hold out no hope of a reprieve, as he would surely hang.

As he awaited execution, George was visited regularly by his family and fiancée, who did not abandon him. Among those who visited the gaol on several occasions was Henry, but during one of the visits George cried out to him, 'Henry, look what you have done to me!' This so upset the youngster that he refused to see his brother again.

During the night of Thursday, 15 August, the eve of his execution, George wrote out a full confession. He died bravely on the following morning before a large crowd outside Derby Gaol.

5

MURDER
IN THE STREET

Chesterfield, 1862

To those who knew him prior to the death of his wife in the summer of 1861, Richard Thorley, who lived in Chesterfield and who worked as a striker at Frost's factory, was a decent, hard working and level headed young man. However, his life was to change in the most dramatic fashion after he met Eliza Morrow, an attractive young Irish woman who worked at Brownsells Mill. A friendship developed, and although Eliza did not want their relationship to become too serious, he became infatuated with her.

Annoyed by what he saw as her rejection of his advances, he assaulted her over the Christmas period of 1861, and although her friends urged her to report the incident to the police, she refused to do so. She had to take time off work due to her injuries, and he gave her the equivalent of one week's wage, 7s 6d, together with three rabbits and a sack of vegetables for her Christmas dinner. She accepted the gifts but made it clear that she wanted nothing more to do with him. However, her decision not to contact the police and to accept the money and food seems to have suggested to his distorted way of thinking that she was fond of him.

Over the next few weeks, he pestered her continuously. He visited her home at 4 Agard Street almost daily, despite her repeatedly telling him to stay away. She told friends that he had threatened to kill her if she would not go out with him, or if he saw her with any other man. He became especially angry when he wrongly suspected that she had formed a relationship with a soldier, in whose company he saw her, but who was in fact her cousin, and who was courting Eliza's friend Kate Griffiths.

Richard Thorley.
(Author's collection)

Thorley began drinking heavily, and it was when very drunk that he went to Eliza's house on the night of Saturday, 8 February 1862. He banged repeatedly on her door, which she opened reluctantly. She demanded that he leave, but he became even more irate when he saw that the soldier was in her house. He refused to leave, and neighbours, concerned for Eliza's safety found a policeman, who managed to persuade Thorley to leave the scene.

The following day, Thorley saw Eliza together with Kate and the soldier, whom he challenged to a fight. However, the soldier ignored him, and, possibly in the hope that it would persuade Thorley to leave her alone, Eliza did not discourage the misconception that the soldier was her lover. She may have believed she had been successful as the next day the group encountered Thorley on the street but he ignored them.

Two days later, on the Tuesday, Eliza did not see Thorley, who was licking his emotional wounds. He drank heavily all day and late into the night. On his way home he became involved in a street fight with a stranger, and was warned by a police officer about his aggressive behaviour. He returned home, and it would emerge later that it was on this night that he sharpened his razor, having decided to murder Eliza.

At midnight on Wednesday, Thorley once again called at Eliza's house, and on this occasion he was beating a drum. He shouted lewd and offensive comments at Eliza and Ann Webster, who lived with her.

Eliza Morrow.
(Author's collection)

He was heard by neighbours to shout that he and the rest of the town knew that the soldier was sharing a bed with the two of them. Eventually, Thorley went home, and once more he spent a considerable amount of time sharpening his razor, and he resolved to return to Agard Street the following night.

At 8 o'clock on the Thursday night, a young boy named Charles Wibberley was playing with a group of friends in Agard Street, outside Eliza's house. He saw her talking to Thorley, and watched as he put his arms around her neck as though in an embrace. Seeing that the youngster was watching, Thorley turned to him and, in a menacing voice, told him to go away.

The boys ran off, but Charles returned unseen, and witnessed Thorley push Eliza against the wall, and as he did so, he heard her scream. Thorley stepped to one side, and Eliza, who was holding her throat, staggered a few feet forward, before falling to the ground. She was lying on her back, and Thorley knelt on top of her briefly before standing, dropping the razor, and running away from the scene. Charles noticed blood on the wall, against which Eliza had been held, and also on the ground. The terrified youngster ran to find help.

The disturbance in the street was heard by Anne Webster and two of her neighbours, Emma Underwood and Uranea Boswell. Anne rushed out into the street as soon as she realised something was amiss. This was moments before Thorley fled, and she ran at him, but the other two women restrained her, as they feared for her safety.

Uranea rushed to Eliza's aid, and at first thought she had simply been knocked down, as she noticed no evidence of wounds or any sign of a blow. Nevertheless, she soon realised the situation was much more serious, and as she tried to lift Eliza, she heard her say, 'May the Lord have mercy on me'. As the two of them stood up, Uranea found that her own clothes and those of Eliza were dripping with blood. Charles Wibberley returned with a police officer who took possession of the razor. He called for assistance from his colleagues and sent for Dr Joseph German, who arrived a few minutes later.

He found the wounded woman lying on a sofa in her home; he could feel no pulse in her wrist, and it was feeble in the carotid artery, which had been exposed by a wound to her neck. He sent for brandy but she died before it arrived. He discovered that the victim had been subjected to a violent and deadly assault, which had resulted in appalling injuries.

There was a wound 4in long, but not very deep, extending from the front of the neck to about one inch behind and below the right ear. This wound joined another across her neck and face, and had exposed a portion of the carotid artery and jugular vein, although these were not damaged. The doctor believed that these wounds were not as serious as they might have been, as Eliza seems to have managed to fend off her attacker successfully, albeit for a brief time only.

A second, much deeper wound, almost 8in long, extended from the right-hand corner of her mouth across the cheek, below the right ear, to the centre of the back of the nape. This wound divided all of the principle veins and arteries and exposed the lower jaw bone, the right side of the base of the skull, and the upper vertebrae of the spine.

Separated from the second, by a narrow strip of skin in the centre of the back of the neck, another major wound, 4in long, extended from the centre of the back of the neck to below the left ear. This led to the left side of the base of the skull and upper vertebrae of the spine being exposed.

Eliza had clearly put up a desperate struggle to defend herself, as the doctor discovered several defensive wounds to her hands and elbows, and there were cuts to the palm of her right hand and the back of the right arm. He believed that the razor found at the scene of the crime was the murder weapon, and this had been responsible for all of her injuries.

The chief constable arrived and organised a search of the town. He also ordered Inspector Fearn to travel to Burton by the turnpike road, and Detective Sergeant Thomas Vessey to travel there by train. Constable Spibey was sent to Nottingham, and Inspector John Green was put in charge of the local search.

As he made his way to the railway station, Detective Sergeant Vessey, who knew Thorley, thought he may have opted to remain in Chesterfield, and he therefore decided to call at a number of public houses to look for him. One of the first he called at was the Spa Inn on Abbey Street, at which the landlord, Thomas Chapman, advised the officer that Thorley had called in at a few minutes past eight o'clock. He had ordered beer and rum, and the landlord had noticed a handkerchief wrapped around his right hand and blood could be seen between his thumb and forefinger. When asked how he had come by the injury, Thorley had replied that he had been fighting a gang of Irishmen in the Abbey Inn. Before leaving the Spa Inn, Thorley had shaken hands with everyone in the establishment and bade them farewell, almost as though he realised he would never return. Suspicious of what he had been told by Thorley, Mr Chapman immediately went to the Abbey Inn, where he was informed there had been no fight similar to that described.

The detective called in several more public houses before eventually spotting Thorley walking towards him, on Canal Street. Thorley recognised the police officer, who said, 'Dick, I want you. I charge you with the murder of that young woman in Agard Street'. To which his prisoner replied, 'Well, I can't help it. I've done it. I'm glad it's you that came to take me, but I won't go till I have lit my cigar'. He continued by saying, 'Well I'm glad on some accounts, but sorry on others'.

Detective Sergeant Vessey took Thorley into the New Inn where he searched him. He noticed dried blood on both of his hands, and in his pockets found three halfpennies, a songbook and some blank paper, all of which were stained with blood. As they left the inn, Thorley, who must have already realised what his probable fate was to be, asked a favour of the officer, 'Let me go up Canal Street, as it may be the last time I shall be able to do so.' His request was granted and the two men walked together along the street as they made their way to the police station.

Within three hours of the crime being committed, Thorley was charged with Eliza's murder by the chief constable. The accused spent the night in the cells before being roused by Inspector Green the following morning with his breakfast. He said, 'Good morning. This is a bad job Dick. How came you did it?' To which Thorley replied, 'I never made my mind up till Tuesday night'.

It had been planned to take the accused man to the magistrates' court in line with normal practice, but news of the murder had spread rapidly, and a large and hostile crowd had gathered in the town centre, making such a journey impossible. It was therefore decided that the magistrates would walk to the police station to hold the first hearing.

Thorley appeared before the magistrates in the Bankruptcy Room of the County Gaol on Thursday, 20 February, and it was at this hearing that he was committed to stand trial at the next assizes for the wilful murder of Eliza. This had also been the outcome of the inquest into her death, which had been held at the Town Hall two days after the crime, before the coroner Mr J. Vallack.

Eliza's funeral took place during the afternoon of the Monday following her death. As usual on such occasions, following a notorious murder, large crowds had assembled along the route from her home to the Nottingham Road Cemetery. Her grave was located in the fourth class ground, next to that of John Harrison, beadle of All Saints' Church, who had also died recently. They were buried simultaneously, and the services in the chapel and at the gravesides were read in alternate portions by the Revds E.W. Foley and J.E. Clarke.

Thorley's trial should have started during the afternoon of Saturday, 22 March 1862 before Mr Justice Williams. However, although Mr Manson and Mr Huish who represented the Crown were present, Mr Yeatman, the defence barrister was nowhere to be seen. As a search for the missing lawyer began, the jury complained to the judge about the delay. Judge Williams decided to wait a further thirty minutes, and during this interval he dealt with another case. This was of Thomas Prime, who was sentenced to one month's imprisonment, having pleaded guilty to an indecent assault. At the conclusion of this case, Mr Yeatman had still not been located, and an angry judge adjourned the trial's start until the following Tuesday. Fortunately for Mr Yeatman, the judge had by then calmed down and accepted his apology, after he explained that on the previous Saturday afternoon he had been told by a member of the court staff that the trial would not be starting that day due to lack of court time.

Thorley pleaded not guilty, and the Crown opened its case by advising the jury that manslaughter was not an appropriate charge in this case, as this was a premeditated and callous murder. The prosecution called the witnesses who had previously given evidence at the inquest and before the magistrates at the committal hearing. The neighbours provided compelling descriptions of the crime; others told of the build up to the murder, especially during the preceding week; and police officers told of Thorley's claims to have decided to kill her on the Tuesday night. Furthermore, the results of the post-mortem proved, the prosecution alleged, that the victim had put up a desperate struggle to save her life, and to have succeeded in inflicting the wounds that he did, Thorley must have been extremely determined to kill her. The motive was clear; if he could not have Eliza, nobody could.

The defence did not cross-examine the prosecution witnesses, and called Thorley to give his account of what had occurred. In a matter-of-fact voice, he told of inflicting the fatal wounds with his razor, and after his client had finished his statement, Mr Yeatman addressed the jury and suggested that although the crime was 'almost murder', the accused was in fact guilty of manslaughter.

To persuade them of this proposition, Mr Yeatman made the best of what he had, as any defence barrister would. He told the jury that they must be satisfied that there was malice aforethought, and that it was a premeditated act. He pointed to the large number of wounds, any one of which could have killed her, and suggested that this indicated he was not acting coolly and deliberately as the Crown was implying, but that he was acting in a passionate frenzy.

As for the Crown's claim that following his arrest he had told police that it was on the Tuesday night that he had decided to kill Eliza later in the week, Mr Yeatman reminded the jury that he had made that alleged statement without the benefit of a solicitor being present; furthermore, no notes had been kept that could be produced at the trial. Thus, he suggested, there were grounds for the jury members to have reasonable doubts as to whether Thorley had described this as a premeditated act, as the police were claiming.

Mr Yeatman also pointed out that following the crime, his client had not fled the town, as the chief constable had thought he would, but rather he remained in the immediate vicinity of the crime, and had surrendered meekly when approached by the arresting officer. This, he proposed, was not what a man who had carefully planned a serious crime would have done.

William Calcraft, who executed Thorley. (The Illustrated Police News)

Finally, the defence barrister called two character witnesses, Thorley's former landlady, and the brother of his late wife. Both spoke of his kindness and his usually placid temperament.

In his detailed summing up, the judge made it clear that he had little sympathy with the defence arguments. He told the jury that there were no grounds for a finding of manslaughter, and if they believed that the accused had killed the victim, there was only one possible verdict, and that was one of wilful murder. The jury took three minutes to decide that they agreed with the prosecution's case, and the judge immediately put on the black cap and sentenced Thorley to death.

Held in Derby Gaol, Thorley seemed resigned to his fate, and as he awaited his execution he spent much of the time in the gaol's chapel and in his cell with the chaplain. He sought solace by reading two pamphlets repeatedly; these were 'A Companion for the Prisoner', published by the Christian Knowledge Society, and the Religious Tract Society's 'The Prisoner's Friend'.

On the eve of his execution he received his last family visit, which lasted two hours, during which he said his farewells to his mother, sisters and brothers. After they left he returned to his cell, where, in the early hours of the morning, he wrote a full confession, which ended:

Ultimately, I committed the act for which I am about to suffer very justly; and I pray God it may be a warning to all, and that God for Christ's sake will pardon my sins which have been many, and particularly that for which I am about to die.

Robert Thorley, 2 a.m. Friday, 11 April 1862

He slept for a few hours before attending chapel for the last time. As he left he bade farewell to the male and female prisoners who had also attended the service, saying, 'Goodbye. Let my fate be a warning to you all'. He joined the procession of prison staff and other officials and walked calmly to his death. He remained composed to the end, and his final act was to shake hands with the executioner, William Calcraft.

He was hanged at noon and died instantly. After the body was cut down, his head was shaved and a death mask made before his burial in the prison grounds. He had no possessions except for a hymnbook, which he left to his sister, and which was inscribed;

Hannah Brierley,
With her brother Richard's dying love.
April 11th 1862.

6

THE GREAT JURY SCANDAL

Derby, 1879

It was a few minutes after four o'clock on the afternoon of Saturday, 12 July 1879, when Constable John Shirley, who was in the Wardwick in Derby, saw a horse and trap being driven towards him at great speed. As the trap approached it swerved violently from side to side, and it was obvious to the officer that it posed a danger to those in its path. As it drew nearer he could see that it was being driven by a well-dressed young man, accompanied by a female passenger, both of whom were clearly drunk.

Concerned for the safety of the couple and others, Constable Shirley stepped off the pavement into the path of the advancing trap, and raising his hand, shouted for the man to stop. The driver ignored his instruction and continued on his way. The officer immediately requisitioned a cab and set off in pursuit. Two of his colleagues, Constables Joseph Moss and John Clamp, had also witnessed the incident, and followed on foot.

The trap slowed down as it neared the Traveller's Rest and turned into the courtyard. Constable Shirley followed a short distance behind, and was joined a few minutes later by his two colleagues.

The police officers found the woman staggering about the courtyard, hopelessly drunk, and the man still sitting in the trap. Shirley removed the reins from the man's grip, before advising him that he was to be arrested for being drunk. To this the man replied, 'It's all right, what are you going to have to drink?' When Shirley replied that he would not be having a drink with him, the man continued, 'It's all right, my father was a magistrate in Staffordshire; come and have something to drink and say no more about it'. Ignoring this offer, Shirley told his prisoner that he would

The shootings. (The Illustrated Police News)

have to accompany him to the police station. The drunk suggested that the constable should 'Jump on behind, I will drive you down'. Shirley, however, ordered him to get down from the trap.

Meanwhile, the other officers were struggling to restrain the woman, who was behaving in an abusive and violent manner. The struggle continued until she fell to the ground, which meant that the three officers were eventually able to arrest her. Shirley had been able to help his colleagues as he had left the man, who was apparently placated, leaning quietly against a wall. The situation now seemingly under control, Clamp and Moss took the inebriated couple to the police office in the cab, and Shirley followed them in the trap.

In the cab however, the woman again began to cause difficulties for the two officers, who were having great problems in keeping her under control. The man shouted out, 'Jesus Christ, I shall have to pay a lot for this. It will cost me £100, but they don't know me, and I shall not tell my name!'

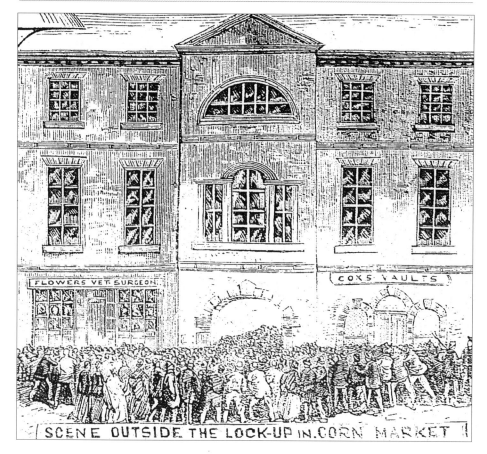

FLOWERS VET SURGEON.

COXS VAULTS

SCENE OUTSIDE THE LOCK-UP IN CORN MARKET

News of the shooting spread quickly and a large crowd gathered outside the lock-up.
(The Illustrated Police News)

Unbeknown to the three police officers, a witness to the events at the Traveller's Rest had been Henry Wibberley, a cab driver. It would emerge later that as the three officers had struggled to control the woman, he had heard the man say in a low but menacing voice, 'If you lay a hand on me, I will shoot you!' This threat had been directed towards the police officers, but none of them had heard him utter the words; if they had, they might possibly have been able to take steps to prevent the tragedy that would soon begin to unfold.

It was half-past four by the time the officers and their prisoners arrived in the police office yard. Constables Clamp and Moss escorted their prisoners into the charge room, which was quite small, and in which Constable Price, the duty officer that afternoon, was sitting at his desk behind the counter. Detective Inspector Ashley Spibey entered the room, and noticed that the male prisoner appeared subdued and was leaning against the counter, whereas the woman was continuing to cause

Constable Moss is carried from the scene of the crime. (The Illustrated Police News)

significant problems for his officers. The inspector shouted to his wife, who was employed by the force as a female searcher, to come and help. His intention was to charge the woman first and place her in a cell so that she could cause no further trouble, and then deal with the man.

Unfortunately this was to prove more difficult than first thought, for she continued to resist furiously. She lashed out and hit Clamp in the face, screaming, 'I will not be locked up!' She managed to struggle free from Moss, Shirley and Spibey, which prompted Price to emerge from behind his desk, shouting, 'We will have none of this!' The number of officers struggling with her was now five, and they almost had her under control when the male prisoner shouted, 'I will have no more of that!' which was followed immediately by a shot.

Constable Moss cried out, 'I am shot!' and his startled colleagues turned to see the prisoner brandishing a revolver. Price rushed at the prisoner, but as he did so the man levelled his gun at him and pulled the trigger. Price fell, clutching his arm, as Spibey and Shirley grappled the man to the floor. However, they were unable to prevent him from firing another shot as they struggled to take the gun from him.

Although drunk, his female companion came to her senses and screamed in terror. She grabbed Clamp's arm, but the officer managed to free himself from her grip and went to the assistance of his colleagues. As he and Shirley grabbed the man by the throat, a fourth shot was fired. Spibey then shouted, 'I have it!' and took possession of the gun, which he handed to his wife.

Having the prisoner under control, the inspector ordered him to be put in a cell, and when Spibey asked him his name the prisoner replied, 'Jeremiah Smith from Jerusalem'. When advised that he was to be charged with shooting two police officers and causing them grievous bodily harm, he declared, 'I would shoot the devil if he was here'.

Lieutenant Colonel William Addis Delacombe, chief constable of the Derby Borough Police Force, was informed of the shootings, and assumed personal charge of the case as soon as he arrived at the police station, where, following a search, he retrieved two of the four bullets that had been fired. The second to have been fired, which had passed through Price's helmet, missing his head by a fraction of an inch, was found lodged in the door which led to the cell area. The fourth shot, which had been fired accidentally during the struggle, was embedded in one of the walls. The first shot had entered Moss's right side, and the third had hit Price in his left arm, and these bullets remained in the victims' bodies.

Colonel Delacombe examined the weapon, which proved to be a five-chambered revolver, in which one bullet remained. Tests would later confirm that this matched the four bullets which had been fired during the incident. The colonel thus possessed strong eyewitness and ballistics evidence.

Finding the still as yet unidentified prisoners too drunk to interview, the colonel made his way to the infirmary to check on the progress of Moss and Price. The latter's wound was 1in above his left elbow, and although none of the main arteries had been severed, he had lost a large quantity of blood. Nevertheless, the wound was not life threatening.

Moss, however, was in a much more serious condition. He was in a state of severe shock, and was experiencing great difficulty in breathing. The bullet had entered 4in below his right nipple and had caused a considerable amount of internal damage. There was little likelihood of his recovering, and it was decided to take a deposition from him. This was witnessed by the colonel and one of the physicians, Dr Taylor, who was also a magistrate.

Colonel Delacombe returned to the police office at 11 p.m. and found that the prisoners had sobered up. The man could remember nothing of

The White Hart Hotel at Ashbourne can be seen on the right-hand side of Church Street. Outside is a horse and trap similar to that hired by Mainwaring. (Author's collection)

the earlier incident, and was shocked to learn he was to be charged with the attempted murder of two police officers.

Meanwhile, at the infirmary, Moss had asked to see his parents, who were brought from their home at Smalley. They remained at his bedside, and despite seeing him rally a little later on the Saturday night, he died the following day at fifteen minutes past noon.

By this time, the police had identified their prisoners. The woman was Annie Green, a local prostitute, and her companion was Gerald Mainwaring. When charged with Moss's murder during the Sunday afternoon, he asked if his victim had been a married man, and he expressed some relief on discovering he had been a bachelor.

A quiet, unassuming and conscientious officer who had been popular with colleagues of all ranks, twenty-six-year-old Moss had joined the force two years earlier. Before that he had served in the Grenadier Guards and remained a member of the Reserves.

The man accused of his murder was the twenty-five-year-old son of the late Revd Mainwaring of Whitmore Hall, Staffordshire, who had served as a magistrate on the Newcastle bench. Despite his high social standing, the prisoner had led a wild and hedonistic lifestyle, which led to plans for him to enter the church as a career having to be abandoned when he was in his youth.

Four years before finding himself in a Derby police cell, facing a murder charge and possible execution, Mainwaring had travelled to North America, where he had become a successful farmer in Manitoba. He had returned to England in mid-April 1879 to spend a few weeks holiday at the home of his two sisters, who lived in Clifton, near Ashbourne. As the time approached for him to return to Manitoba, he had decided to spend a few days in Derby, where he could enjoy himself in his own particular manner, away from the restrictive atmosphere of his sisters' home.

Having hired a horse and trap from the White Hart in Ashbourne on the previous Tuesday, he had booked in at the Royal Hotel on his arrival in Derby. He spent the following days drinking heavily, and spent a great deal of time in the company of Annie Green, who lived in a brothel on Bradshaw Street. This had supposedly been closed down by the police some months earlier, but its owner, Sophia Gilbert, had reopened the premises in the guise of a cigar shop.

Mainwaring's money had soon run out and he was forced to pawn his watch and five rings to finance his stay for a few days more. He decided to return to Ashbourne on the afternoon of Saturday, 12 July.

It was during his stay in Derby that Mainwaring had bought the gun used in the shootings of the police officers, for £3 10s, at the Market Place premises of Messrs Dobson and Rosson. Mrs Euphemia Dobson, who sold it to him, later told the police that Mainwaring also had in his possession the chamber of a Colt revolver, for which he purchased 300 rounds of ammunition, together with 200 rounds for the new weapon. Mainwaring told Mrs Dobson that he would need both guns for use when he returned to North America in a few days time.

On the day of the crime, he and Annie Green began drinking heavily in the morning, and both were drunk by the early afternoon. He ordered his horse and trap to be made ready, and the couple left at 3.15 p.m.

Mainwaring asked Annie Green to accompany him to Clifton, but she was reluctant to do so, and he agreed to take her back to Mrs Gilbert's premises. There, she got out of the trap, and as she staggered towards the front door, he had a change of mind. He too approached the door, which had been opened by Mrs Gilbert. He insisted that the young woman accompany him, but Mrs Gilbert would not let her go, telling him 'I insist she shall not go out, she is in so beastly a state'.

Mainwaring, however, was not to be so easily persuaded, and as he pulled out his gun, which he kept down by his side, he retorted, 'Now will you let her go?' Mrs Gilbert was not initially intimidated, as she replied, 'No, let her lie down and have a sleep, and then go out if you wish'.

Mainwaring, however, was not to be denied. He grabbed hold of his paramour, and pointed the gun at Mrs Gilbert, who cried out, 'Oh for God's sake, he is going to shoot me! Take her and go!'

A neighbour, Harry Harrison, disturbed by the fracas, emerged from his front door to see the gun being pointed at Mrs Gilbert. As Mainwaring climbed back into the trap, Mr Harrison pointed to the gun and said,

'You had better put that thing away'. Mainwaring glared at him, and shouted menacingly, 'I have shot better than you!' He drove off but would be arrested just a few minutes later at the Traveller's Rest.

Mainwaring appeared in the local police court on two occasions; these were on the Monday and Wednesday following the shootings, before he was committed by the magistrates to stand trial at the next assizes. It had been decided that there were insufficient grounds to charge Annie Green with any involvement in the shootings, but she appeared in the police court on Monday, 14 July, charged with being drunk and also with assaulting Constable Clamp.

At the hearing she claimed to remember nothing of the events of the previous Saturday afternoon. Nevertheless, she accepted the evidence given by the police officers. However, she pointed to her badly blackened eye, and suggested that anything she had done would probably have been in response to the rough manner in which she claimed she was handled by the police. After giving the matter some thought, Colonel Delacombe withdrew the assault charge, and she was therefore convicted only of being drunk. The magistrates fined her 10s or fourteen days' imprisonment in default. She had no means of paying and was taken to Derby Gaol.

The inquest into Moss's death was held on Tuesday, 15 July in the boardroom of the infirmary, before Mr J. Close, the county coroner. The accused was not present, but he was represented by local solicitor, Mr Hextall. Present in court were Mainwaring's brother and Constable Moss's distraught mother and sister.

Colonel Delacombe outlined the case against the accused, and two particularly powerful statements were read out to the jury. The first was a brief description of the post-mortem findings, which gave graphic details of the devastating impact of the bullet which killed Moss, and the second was the reading of the victim's deposition, taken as he lay dying.

The post-mortem had been performed by the infirmary's acting surgeon, Hugh Redmayne. After describing the failed attempts to save the officer's life, the jury was told that the bullet had passed through his ribs, badly damaging his liver and gall bladder.

The chief constable next read the dead man's deposition to a hushed room:

I was in the police office, about half past four, and I assisted to take two prisoners into the station house. One was a man and the other was a woman. I was standing close to the man, when the other officers were taking the woman into the cells. The man lifted a revolver up and said 'Stand back, I'll have no more of this'. I heard a report, and I felt a shot in my right side, and fell down. I said 'I am shot'.

The Corn Market, where the funeral procession was held up due to the large number of Derby residents wishing to pay their respects to Constable Moss. (Author's collection)

Inspector Spibey and Constables Price, Shirley and Clamp were present. I remember nothing until I found myself here. I heard three reports of a shot, two after I was shot. I make this declaration believing that I am about to die.

Mr Hextall had attempted to prevent the deposition being read out at the inquest, but the coroner allowed it, pointing out that such death-bed statements were acceptable and crucial pieces of evidence. Mr Close further advised the jury to ignore the defence claims that Mainwaring's judgement had been impaired as he was drunk. The coroner emphasised that if he had been under the influence of alcohol, it would not excuse the crime or reduce the level of seriousness in any way. The jury retired for ten minutes before returning with their verdict. They decided that Constable Moss had been the victim of wilful murder, and Mainwaring was sent for trial on a coroner's warrant.

While Mainwaring languished in Derby Gaol, Constable Moss's funeral took place on Friday, 18 July. Several thousand people from Derby and much further afield lined the route from the infirmary grounds to the cemetery. The body was placed in a polished oak coffin, which bore a brass plate inscribed: 'Joseph Moss, died July 13th 1879, aged 26'. The coffin was placed in a glass-sided hearse, and draped in a Union Jack flag, on which a number of wreaths were placed.

"England expects that every man will do his duty."

In Memory
OF

JOSEPH MOSS,
OF THE

DERBY BOROUGH POLICE FORCE
(Formerly of the Grenadier Guards,)

AGED 26 YEARS,

WHO WAS SHOT, JULY 12, 1879,

Whilst in the Execution of his Duty,
and died next day.

———

BURIED AT THE NOTTINGHAM ROAD CEMETERY

With Military Honours.

The funeral card of Constable Moss. (Derbyshire County Council, Derbyshire Police Collection)

Members of the Derby Borough Police and the Derbyshire County Force were present in large numbers, and many officers from the neighbouring Nottingham force, including its band, also attended. All of these officers had paid their own travel expenses, and many had worked through the previous night, so had not yet slept. Each officer wore black crape on his left arm as a mark of respect.

In view of the deceased's past military service, an invitation had been extended to any serving military personnel who were in the town at the time. Two non-commissioned officers from the Grenadier Guards responded to the invitation, and took a leading role in the cortège. Sergeant Coney and Corporal Minns made a splendid sight in their distinctive busbies, and received a warm response from those lining the route. Members of the watch committee, representatives of the town council and many of the borough's magistrates were also present. The chief mourners, however, were members of the dead officer's family, and these were his parents, William and Louisa, his siblings John, Lillie and Louisa, along with a cousin and four aunts.

The crowd was so dense in the Corn Market that the procession was delayed for some time, while a path through was cleared. At the cemetery, the coffin was carried into the chapel between ranks of the late constable's uniformed colleagues, and the service was conducted by Revd F.J. Lyall, vicar of St Luke's.

Such was the interest in Mainwaring's trial, which was held at the Derby Assizes on 1 August 1879, that a huge downpour of rain did not deter a large crowd from besieging the court building. However, admission was by ticket only, so that most of the crowd were left outside, disappointed as well as drenched.

At 10 a.m. the trial judge, Mr Justice Lindley, took his seat; the prosecution was led by Mr Lawrence QC, who was assisted by Horace Smith; the defendant was represented by the Solicitor General, Sir Hardinge Giffard QC MP, and Mr Harris. When the charges of the wilful murder of Constable Moss, and the attempted murder of Constable Price were formally put to him, Mainwaring pleaded not guilty to both matters.

The prosecution's first witness was Fanny Davis, a waitress at the Royal Hotel. She testified that the accused had drunk heavily throughout his stay, and this was especially so on the morning of the day on which the shootings occurred. Next, Sophia Gilbert and Joseph Harrison described his threatening behaviour that day, when he insisted that Annie Green accompany him to his sisters' home. The police officers on duty on the day of the shootings, including Constable Price, whose arm was still in a sling, described the chase through Derby and the events which took place in the charge room. Henry Wibberley told of hearing Mainwaring's threat to shoot the officers, and medical evidence was given of the wounds suffered by the two victims. Finally, the deathbed deposition of Constable Moss was read out in court.

The defence could clearly not attempt to persuade the jury that their client was not responsible for shooting both officers, and they called no witnesses other than two of his former school masters, a vicar and an old family servant, to testify to his more positive qualities. Nor was the Solicitor General especially aggressive in his cross-examinations of the prosecution witnesses. Instead, he focused solely on the issue of his client's drunken state. It was under his questioning that Fanny Davis revealed to an astonished court that with their breakfasts on that fateful Saturday morning, Mainwaring and his female companion had between them drunk three pints of claret and a quart bottle of brandy. His questioning of the police officers revealed that they all believed that Mainwaring had been extremely drunk from the moment of his arrest, until much later that night. Colonel Delacombe acknowledged this when he described finding it impossible to question his prisoner for several hours, and told the court how at one stage he had found the prisoner lying on the floor of his cell rambling incoherently.

The prosecution realised that the defence was attempting to persuade the jury that Mainwaring had been so drunk that he had not been fully responsible for his actions. Therefore, in his final address to the jury, Mr Lawrence stressed that the Crown considered him to have been master of his own actions, and that no one had the right to incapacitate him or herself through alcohol, and later use this as an excuse for any criminal act.

Sir Hardinge did indeed claim that Mainwaring's drunken state was a critical issue, and should be taken into account when determining his fate. For instance, there had been no malice aforethought, and the fact that the shootings had taken place in a room full of police officers demonstrated that he could not have realised what he was doing, nor could he have been aware of the consequences of his actions. Sir Hardinge did not suggest that his client did not deserve to be punished for his crimes, but insisted that he should be convicted of manslaughter and not wilful murder.

In his summing up the judge gave the jury a clear direction on the issue of the accused's drunken state. He emphasised that it had been established some years earlier in law that being drunk could not excuse murder, and it could not be used as a reason for reducing the charge to manslaughter.

The jury retired at 1 p.m., returning three hours and twenty minutes later. They had found Mainwaring guilty of murder, but added a strong recommendation for mercy. Mr Justice Lindley sentenced him to death, and advised him that he would pass the jury's recommendation to the Home Secretary, but in view of the nature of the crime, he should not expect to be reprieved.

As the jury would become one of the most notorious in legal history, not because of their verdict, but the manner in which it was reached, it is worth recording their names. They were; Charles Astle, John Halliday, John Wood, Vincent Shepherd, Francis Ludlow, Joseph Mitchell Tempest, Henry Kent, John Pym Stevens, John Stevenson, Samuel Burton, John Bromley and William Sheldon.

On Monday, 4 August, the murder trial having ended, Derby Member of Parliament, Sir Wilfrid Lawson raised the case in the House of Commons. He asked the Home Secretary, Richard Assheton Cross, whether consideration had been given to prosecuting the landlord of the Royal Hotel, in view of the details that had emerged at the trial. The Home Secretary confirmed that the landlord, John Taylor, would indeed face prosecution, and that furthermore he would be appearing before the Derby Magistrates on the following Thursday.

At that hearing, John Taylor appeared before the local bench to face a charge of permitting drunkenness on his premises, to which he pleaded not guilty. His solicitor was Mr Briggs, who complained that the public notoriety given to the matter by Sir Wilfred was unfair and unwarranted, and his client had done nothing wrong. The magistrates did not agree with this argument, finding the landlord guilty and fining him £3.

Another piece of unfinished business that could now be concluded was to acknowledge Constable Price's bravery. Many townspeople felt that this deserved public recognition, and ten of Derby's leading citizens each donated £1 towards a collection for him. The officer was presented with the £10 by the mayor, W.J. Smith, in a ceremony at the police court. This was intended to be a contribution towards the cost of a holiday to help in his recovery, and he informed those assembled at the presentation that he would be going to stay with friends in Kent.

It was about this time that rumours began to circulate about the manner in which the jury had reached its verdict. On 6 August, a Sheffield newspaper claimed that six members of the jury had wanted to convict Mainwaring of manslaughter, whereas the remainder had favoured a conviction for murder. To end this deadlock and reach a verdict, they were alleged to have drawn lots, and the member who drew a blank card would decide what the verdict would be. It was also reported that the jury member who drew that card had actually favoured a verdict of manslaughter, but decided to opt for a murder conviction in deference to the feelings of those who favoured such a finding. The differences in the jury room were said to have arisen from a feeling shared by six of them that the judge's guidance notwithstanding, and despite the very serious nature of the offences, they had not been premeditated acts, and Mainwaring had behaved in a manner he would not have done if he had been sober.

On 11 August, Charles Astle, a wheelwright of Aston-on-Trent, made a public statement in which he attempted to explain what had occurred. He stated:

> After retiring from the box, I found that there were six in favour of a verdict of murder, and a similar number in favour of a verdict of manslaughter. Perhaps I might add that my own views were in favour of the latter. After a considerable time, the discussion was so very wearisome and desultory, that it was decided among us to elect a chairman, I having refused to act. None of the jurymen would consent to occupy the position, and eventually we decided to cast lots for who was to be the chairman. Accordingly this was done, but as to drawing lots or tossing up as to the verdict we were to return, that is a tissue of falsehoods and without the slightest shadow of foundation.

This, however, did not put an end to the matter, especially as it later emerged that when Mr Astle was asked by the Home Office for an explanation of what had occurred in the jury room, he gave a different version of events. In this he confirmed that the jury members decided that a majority of them would decide upon the verdict, and if the numbers were equal, the chairman chosen by ballot would have the deciding vote.

There was a widespread sense of incredulity that it could be left to just one man in effect, to more or less decide on the fate of a man on trial for his life. The behaviour of the Mainwaring jury was considered by many to be contrary to the basic features of trial by ones peers, in which a verdict should be agreed by all of the members of the jury and should be reached by rational means, based on evidence presented in court. Some called for a retrial while others believed that there should at least be a reprieve for Mainwaring.

Other members of the jury entered the debate, and Henry Kent blamed Mr Astle, whom he believed had refused to carry out the responsibilities of jury foreman, which led to the need for a ballot to select one. He insisted that there had been no deciding vote, and that before leaving the jury room, each jury member had agreed with the murder verdict.

Joseph Mitchell Tempest claimed that the initial vote had been split evenly, but one of their number wavered and this meant there was a majority of seven to five favouring a murder verdict. After further fruitless discussion and Mr Astle's refusal to act as chairman, it was decided to cast lots for the position. Nevertheless, he was adamant that this was not done with a view to having a deciding vote. He further insisted that their discussions had led to all of the jury members favouring a murder verdict.

However, there was a widespread feeling that although differing accounts had been given by some jury members, they had acted inappropriately. There remained the suspicion that those who had changed their positions to favouring a finding of murder had not done so because of rational argument heard in the courtroom, but rather to simply break the deadlock. It was clear that the Home Secretary could not ignore the situation as he decided upon the fate of Mainwaring.

As the controversy continued, a petition was started by Mr Hextall, which read as follows:

> The humble petition and memorials of the undersigned inhabitants of Derby showeth;
> 1. That we have read the reports of the trial at the Derby Assizes, on the 31st day of July 1879 of Gerald Mainwaring for the wilful murder of Joseph Moss.
> 2. That having regard to the state of complete drunkenness under which the said Gerald Mainwaring suffered at the time he committed the act which resulted in the death of the deceased man, Moss, we feel compelled to express our thorough belief that the said Gerald Mainwaring was not at the time conscious of what would be the probable effects of the act he did, and that the said act was in that sense involuntary on his part.
> 3. That we believe the said Gerald Mainwaring had no deliberate intentions of doing harm to any person.
> 4. We believe that in the above expressions of opinion we correctly represent the sentiments of an overwhelming majority of those who have carefully read the reports of the said trial.
> Your petitioners therefore humbly pray that you will be pleased to advise Her Majesty to remit the sentence of death under which the said Gerald Mainwaring now lies, and your petitioners will ever pray.

Another local man, Thomas Spooner Litherland, had been sentenced to death for the murder of his wife at the same assizes as Mainwaring. He was well known in the town and it was recognised that there was a history of mental illness in his family, and that he had suffered similarly. There was thus a great deal of support favouring a reprieve for him also. A mass public meeting was held in the Market Place on Thursday, 7 August, which was addressed by the Revd W. Wilkinson and Councillor Holmes. The petitions in favour of reprieves for both men, who were due to be hanged together on the following Monday morning, were sent for the Home Secretary to consider.

A total of 5,720 signed Mainwaring's petition, and given the difficult situation the jury's behaviour had placed him in, it came as no surprise when the Home Secretary decided that Mainwaring would not stand on the scaffold of Derby Gaol, and his sentence was commuted to one of life imprisonment. Litherland was also reprieved and sent to Broadmoor Criminal Lunatic Asylum. Mainwaring served fifteen years in prison and was released on licence in May 1894.

7

A MURDER OF SINGULAR ATROCITY

Derby, 1880

James Wilkinson earned his living by making comb-boxes, and in March 1880, having recently moved from Newcastle, he was living at 67 Bridge Street in Derby with his wife, son and two daughters. His eldest daughter Elizabeth, who was sixteen years old, hawked her father's comb-boxes, which cost one penny each, from door to door. James decided that it was time that his youngest daughter Eliza, who had celebrated her eighth birthday on 8 February, help her sister sell his wares.

At nine o'clock on the morning of Monday, 26 April, Eliza left the family home with Elizabeth for only the second time. The eldest girl had thirteen of her father's comb-boxes to sell, and Eliza had just one. Within three hours this poor but happy and loving family would be devastated by what a local journalist described as 'a shocking murder, committed under circumstances of singular atrocity'.

One hour after leaving home, there were only two comb-boxes left to sell, and the girls found themselves on Green Street. Each took one of the comb-boxes and chose the houses each would call at, and agreed to meet when they had called at all of the houses or sold the boxes. At eleven o'clock, having waited several minutes for her sister, Elizabeth decided to go and look for her. She knocked on several doors along the route Eliza would have taken, and at one of the houses, Mary Ann Keeling informed her that Eliza had called at her house a few minutes earlier, and after telling her she did not wish to buy anything, she watched as the little girl walked down a passage leading off Green Street and into Tan Yard.

Elizabeth entered the yard but as there was no sign of her sister, she decided to go home in case she had made her own way back. Finding that she was

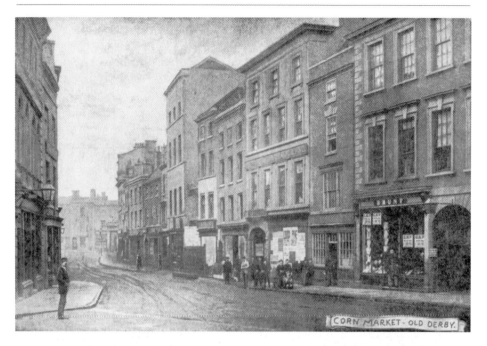

James Wilkinson moved to Derby with his young family with high hopes, but suffered a great tragedy. (Author's collection)

not there, her brother James left with Elizabeth to search for their sister once again. Their parents remained in the house in case Eliza returned there.

As the brother and sister reached Green Street, they were approached by a woman who knew them, to say that a young girl fitting their sister's description had just been murdered. They rushed to Tan Yard where they were met by the imposing figure of the town's chief constable, Colonel William Addis Delacombe, who told James to return home and advise his parents to come as quickly as possible. Eliza's father arrived soon afterwards, and following a brief discussion with the chief constable and Detective Inspector Spibey, he was led into one of the nearby dwellings, 1 Court House. There, the devastated father was confronted by the sight of his youngest daughter's lifeless body.

The house in which the body had been discovered was the home of the Wakefield family, and it had been John Wakefield, who lived there with his widowed mother and brother, who a few minutes earlier had walked into the nearby police station. He had approached the desk, where he told Inspector Barnes, 'I want to see the superintendent very particularly'. When asked for what reason, he replied, 'I have committed a murder'.

However, Wakefield appeared to be so calm and unconcerned as he spoke, that the inspector did not initially believe him, and thought that he was one of those odd individuals who occasionally visited the station,

John Wakefield. (The Illustrated Police News)

Tan Yard, off Green Street, where the terrible crime took place. (The Illustrated Police News)

claiming to have committed a terrible crime simply to draw attention to themselves. However, Wakefield persisted by saying, 'This is not a fallacy, it's true.' The inspector remained sceptical but summoned Colonel Delacombe, who questioned Wakefield more closely. Wakefield persisted with his claim, stating, 'I have committed a murder at my mother's house. You had better go and see for yourself.'

Colonel Delacombe did so, and, finding Eliza's body lying in one of the downstairs rooms, discovered that Wakefield's account was true. Having broken the news to her father, the chief constable returned to the police station where, on the strength of his spoken confession, he charged Wakefield with the murder.

The scene of the crime was a horrific sight. Eliza, whose throat had been cut, was lying on her back in a large pool of blood at the bottom of the stairs, which led to the bedrooms. Still wearing her bonnet, her head was turned towards the right side, and in her hand she was holding a halfpenny. Close to the body was a dinner knife, covered with blood, and the comb-box she had hoped to sell when calling at the house, was on a table, upon which there was a bowl of freshly peeled potatoes. In a corner of the room was a bucket full of water which was red with blood, suggesting to the police that Wakefield had washed his hands in it after committing the murder.

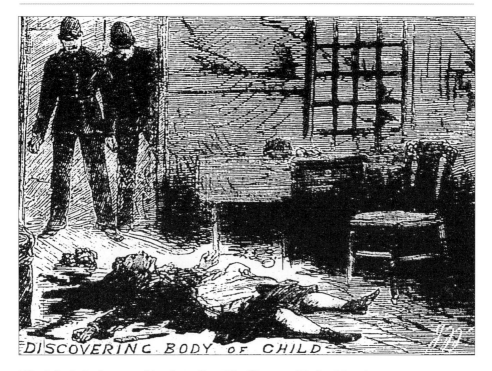

Eliza's body is discovered by the police. (The Illustrated Police News)

It was quickly surmised that Eliza must have knocked on the door, and had been enticed in by her killer by the promise of a halfpenny for the comb-box. Once inside the house, she had been murdered almost immediately.

Other evidence incriminating their prisoner was discovered when Wakefield was searched by Sergeant Joseph Stewartson, who found bloodstains on the left sleeve of his shirt, and although he had washed his hands following the crime, dried blood remained under his fingernails.

Colonel Delacombe had called for Dr Sharpe to attend the murder scene, and he found the body to be still warm. There were two knife wounds to the right side of the neck. However, he would discover later, having performed a post-mortem, that it was two wounds to the left side of the neck that had been the cause of death. One of these had severed her windpipe, and the knife had entered the gullet. One had been struck with such force that the point of the knife had emerged from the opposite side of the little girl's neck. The jugular vein had been severed and death had almost certainly been instantaneous.

The doctor found another knife wound to her right shoulder which had not been fatal, and which had probably resulted from the struggle Eliza had put up before being overpowered by her killer. There were also bruises to her knees and elbows, and another on her upper right arm. At the chief constable's request, the doctor examined the body for any signs of rape, and although there was a small bruise on her abdomen, there was no evidence that a sexual crime had been committed.

Thirty-year-old John Wakefield, the man being held on suspicion of murdering Eliza, had a reputation for being lazy, with an aversion to work, and of being a rather strange individual. A loner, it had been seven years since his last job, and when his mother and brother, Arthur, were out at work during the day, he would perform household tasks such as washing and shopping. He read constantly, especially the Bible, and visited the Free Library every day. When his mother and brother returned in the evening John would go to bed.

He was given to violent outbursts, and his family were said to be extremely frightened of him at such times. On one occasion his brother reported finding a rope suspended in the suspect's bedroom as though he had been contemplating suicide, but Arthur removed it before it could be used.

The police had no other avenues to investigate, as they had the prisoner's confession together with overwhelming circumstantial evidence. However, they could find no motive for the crime, as there were no signs of rape or attempted sexual contact, and Elizabeth confirmed that she had all of the cash from their sales that morning, which excluded robbery as a reason for the crime. Furthermore, Wakefield had been sober at the time the murder was committed, so alcohol was not a contributory factor to the vicious attack.

Wakefield appeared before the magistrates in a crowded court the following day. Throughout the proceedings he appeared unconcerned at what was happening around him. The chief constable provided sufficient information to demonstrate a *prima facie* case against the accused, and sought an adjournment so that further enquiries could be made, and also to allow sufficient time for the inquest to take place. The case was therefore adjourned until the following Thursday.

The inquest was held on the following day in the Guildhall's Grand Jury Room. Having listened to the police evidence and the details provided of her wounds, the jury took only three minutes to find that Eliza had been murdered by John Wakefield. At the adjourned hearing before the magistrates, he was also committed to stand trial at the Derby Assizes. He appeared disinterested at both of these hearings and ignored the loud hisses from those in the courtroom that greeted his removal from the dock.

Eliza's funeral took place on the same day as the second hearing before the magistrates, and the cost was paid by Mr Sutton, the son of the landlord of the house in which the Wilkinsons were living. The body had been taken from the mortuary to the house on Bridge Street, from where the procession started its sad journey. The entire route to the Nottingham Road Cemetery was thronged with thousands of people, and there was a large crowd at the graveside, all of whom experienced an intensely emotional occasion.

Wakefield's trial took place before Baron Huddleston on Thursday, 29 July, and J.H. Etherington-Smith prosecuted. Wakefield, who pleaded not guilty, had insufficient funds to employ an advocate to act on his behalf. The judge therefore asked Mr Stranger to represent the prisoner, and despite the lack of time he had to prepare his case, the barrister represented his newly acquired client as best he could.

The Crown opened by telling the jury that although there had been no eyewitness to the crime, there was overwhelming circumstantial evidence against the man in the dock. It was acknowledged that the Crown could not provide a motive for the crime, but emphasised that it was not necessary to do so.

The jury listened intently to the testimony of the deceased's sister, the police officers to whom Wakefield had made his confession, and the medical evidence, all of which went largely unchallenged by the defence. Instead, Mr Stranger, who did not attempt to suggest that his client had not killed Eliza, opted for a defence of insanity. Despite the short time spent on the case, he arranged for Dr Wright Baker, surgeon at Derby Gaol to attend the trial. The doctor testified that during his career he had met many murderers who committed motiveless crimes under an uncontrollable impulse. The judge intervened by stating that every act was done under some form of impulse or other.

Ignoring the judge's interruption, the doctor continued his testimony by stating that in his opinion Wakefield had acted under such an impulse, and he highlighted the absence of a motive, the absence of any attempt at concealment of the crime, and the lack of interest shown by the prisoner at previous hearings, which was also evident from his demeanour during the trial.

At the conclusion of the evidence, both advocates addressed the jury. Mr Stranger insisted that his client was insane, and all of the features of the murder, and the defendant's subsequent behaviour, suggested that he had not been responsible for his actions. Mr Etherington-Smith simply pointed to the overwhelming evidence against him and the absence of any proof that he was insane.

In his summing up, Baron Huddleston focused on the issue of Wakefield's state of mind at the time of the murder. He urged the jury not to be misled by what he described as fanciful theories. He referred to what he described as Dr Baker's startling theory, and asked what was the meaning of a so-called uncontrollable impulse. He had said it stemmed from a lack of self-control, but that, the judge continued, was the case with any crime that was committed. As far as the prisoner was concerned, there was no proof of any hereditary insanity, and it would therefore be unwise to give the doctor's theory any credibility.

If people always controlled their passions, the judge argued, there would be no crime. However, it was because people lost control that gave rise to the promptings of their evil nature, that crimes, including murder, were committed. If people who could not control their passions were not to be punished, because of a lack of self-control, lunatic asylums would have to be built across the nation rather than prisons. Furthermore, rather than juries deciding the fate of an accused, it would be doctors doing so.

His duty, he continued, was to tell the jury what the law stated. Every accused individual was presumed to be sane unless the contrary was shown to be the case, based on evidence presented at the trial. The process for deciding if an accused person was sane or otherwise had been laid down by the House of Lords. This meant that the jury had to decide whether the accused had a sufficient degree of reason to know that he or she was doing wrong. If satisfied that the answer was in the affirmative, the jury must convict him.

The jury deliberated for ten minutes before returning with a guilty verdict, and there was no recommendation for mercy. The judge donned his black cap and told Wakefield:

> Prisoner at the bar, I do not wish to add to your misery at this moment. What was your object in taking away the life of this happy little girl must to most minds be a matter of conjecture. That you bargained with her for that little comb-box, gave her that halfpenny and that you then murdered her in the most brutal manner, and then simply by conscience gave yourself up, is all we know of the facts. I have but one duty to perform; it is incumbent upon me in the position I hold, but as a fellow man, let me ask you to avail yourself of the time that is left before the sentence of the court is carried out, to prepare yourself to meet your Maker. Repentance is open to you, and that is now your only prospect. The sentence of the Court upon you for the crime of wilful murder of which you have now been convicted, is that you be taken from this place where you are now to the prison from whence you came, and that on a day appointed you shall be taken to a suitable place of execution and be there hanged by the neck.

It was clear from the judge's comments that the prospect of a reprieve was negligible. However, despite this and the absence of a recommendation for mercy, a petition to save Wakefield's life was started. It was drawn up by his solicitor, Mr Wheatcroft, who continued to claim that his client was insane, using new information provided by Wakefield's mother. She also wrote a personal letter to the Home Secretary claiming that in the weeks leading up to the murder, she had noticed that her son had been acting in a peculiar manner. He had gone several days without eating, and there had been a number of violent outbursts for no apparent reason. She believed this gave credence to the claim that her son was insane, and that the crime had resulted from an uncontrollable impulse. If the jury had been aware of this information, she believed a different verdict might have been reached.

There was some support for the petition, and among those who signed it were several of the town's magistrates, members of the Town Council, a number of local ministers, and one of the jury members who had found Wakefield guilty. However, the Home Secretary was unmoved and the petition failed. The execution was scheduled for Monday, 16 August.

Following his conviction, Wakefield was visited on just two occasions by his mother and brother, who did so for the last time on the Saturday afternoon before his execution. They had great difficulty in coming to terms with what he had done, but he refused to answer their questions about the crime. The executioner, William Marwood, also arrived at the gaol that afternoon.

On the eve of his execution, Wakefield went to bed early and seemed to be sleeping well, but at one o'clock in the morning he awoke suffering from a terrible toothache, which lasted throughout the night. He dressed at 5 a.m., and ate a light breakfast two hours later. Just before 8 a.m., the prison officials arrived to accompany him to the scaffold. He retained his composure throughout, and the execution was carried out without incident. Within minutes of the black flag being raised, the crowd outside the gaol, which was estimated to number 2,000, dispersed. While Wakefield was being buried, Marwood left the gaol, unnoticed, by a side door.

Since his arrest Wakefield had given no indication as to a motive for the crime, saying nothing to the police, his family or his lawyers. However, a few days before he was hanged he told Revd Moore that he had grown tired of life but did not have the courage to commit suicide. He had therefore decided to commit a crime so heinous that his own death, at the hands of the hangman, would inevitably follow.

The Wakefield case was the cause of a dispute between two local newspapers, which was as fierce as any involving today's tabloids. Since public executions had been abolished in 1868, the governors of those prisons at which hangings took place had the authority to decide on the number of journalists who could attend them. By 1880, the Home Office was discouraging the presence of the press at executions, as their reports focused on the distressing scenes on the scaffold and other unfortunate mishaps that sometimes occurred on such occasions.

The governor of Derby Gaol had decided to invite just one reporter to Wakefield's hanging, from the *Derby Daily Telegraph*, who, it was proposed, could provide an account for other newspapers to use. However, this infuriated rival publication the *Derby Mercury*, which accused the editor of its fierce rival of having resorted to sharp practice in order to obtain the invitation, and it complained bitterly to the governor. This appears to have had the desired effect as journalists from all of the local newspapers were invited to executions until the practice finally stopped several years later.

8

THE DROWNING OF
A LOVED ONE

Bonsall, 1880

In May 1877 Mary Wright, a single young woman, gave birth to an illegitimate daughter, Adeline. The baby's father had deserted Mary when first told of the pregnancy. However, her family remained supportive and she did not therefore have to consider the dangerous option of an illegal abortion, the tragedy of infanticide, or entry into the workhouse, which were the choices facing many women in her situation in Victorian England. Her father, James, was a wealthy farmer who owned twenty acres of good farmland on Bonsall Moor, where he lived with his wife and two other daughters, Alice and Elizabeth.

All went well for the next three years, as not only did her family provide Mary and Adeline with a loving home, but their neighbours did not ostracise Mary and they also became very fond of Adeline. However, Mary's seducer returned to the area, and such was her infatuation she feared she was once again pregnant by this man. When she told him that she bore his second child, he again abandoned her and refused to face up to his responsibilities, and absconded for a second time.

For weeks she worried what she should do, until at breakfast on Sunday, 4 July 1880 Mary broke the news to her appalled father. This was too much for him to bear, and in a rage he accused her of bringing shame on the family. He insisted that she make arrangements to leave the family home as soon as possible, and that she would have to take Adeline with her. A subdued Mary told him she and the child would leave, as he wished. Given the age in which they lived, her father's reaction was perhaps understandable, but this outburst and its aftermath would no doubt haunt him until the end of his days.

Bonsall. (Author's collection)

Following the confrontation with her father, Mary went to her room, taking Adeline with her. She remained there for several hours until 5.30 p.m., when she left the house with her daughter to milk her father's cows. Two hours later her father saw her and his granddaughter from a distance, walking towards Grange Mill. The distance between them was too great for him to speak to Mary, but he presumed she was going to her uncle's house, which she visited regularly. However, he would learn in just a few hours that this was a mistaken belief, and he was unaware at the time that, before leaving the house earlier, Mary had left a letter addressed to her mother in which she gave details of her plans, and which would only be found some hours later.

Mary spent the next few hours wandering about the district, and was seen by a number of people who knew her. Cousins William and Thomas Bunting were out for an evening stroll and met Mary and Adeline. As they passed, William teased her by calling out, 'Mary, you will be getting lost up here'. She replied that she knew the lanes too well to become lost. Both men described her as being apparently cheerful, without any worries seemingly preying on her mind. One hour later, she was seen carrying Adeline in her arms by another friend, John Worthy, who later would also say that she seemed to be in good spirits.

Mary's parents and sisters went to bed at half-past ten and although Mary and Adeline had not returned home, they believed she must have decided to spend the night at her uncle's home at Grange Mill, which she had done on several occasions in the past. Sadly, this would prove not to be the case.

Mary Wright. (National Archives)

Henry and Elizabeth Spencer lived fifty yards from the Wright's farmhouse, and knew all of the family very well. Shortly before midnight, Mrs Spencer was woken by loud knocking at her front door. When she opened it she was surprised to find Mary standing alone in the porch, and who in a calm voice asked if she could come inside. She was drenched from head to foot, and Mrs Spencer looked outside to see if it was raining, but it was not. Mary told her that she was wet because she had been in the pond in one of her father's fields. She then added that she had left Adeline there, and Mrs Spencer noticed that her visitor was carrying the child's bonnet and shawl, both of which she recognised.

An alarmed Mrs Spencer rushed to Mary's home, which she found in darkness. Her repeated shouting and knocking at the door eventually roused the young woman's parents, and James appeared at the bedroom window. Mrs Spencer explained that Mary was at her home, and he and his wife should come immediately as it seemed that something was terribly wrong. When the Wrights arrived at their neighbour's home they found Mary standing by the fire drying herself and trying to keep warm. Her mother was by now weeping as she realised instinctively that something dreadful must have occurred. She asked Mary where Adeline was, to which Mary replied, 'Don't cry mother, as no one is to blame but me'. Mrs Wright wrapped her arms protectively around Mary's shoulders and took her home. Meanwhile, James and Henry ran to the field in which the pond was located.

When they reached the pond the moon was hidden behind clouds, and it was so dark that the two men could see nothing. They both waded into the pond, which was just 3ft deep in the middle. They felt under the water, and after a few minutes, Henry felt something under the surface, and he lifted the small lifeless body of Adeline from out of the freezing pond. The men wrapped her in a shawl before making their way to the Wrights' home. One can only imagine what thoughts were going through the mind of the little girl's grandfather, who a few hours earlier had ordered his daughter and her child out of his house.

By the time they arrived at the house, Mary had been put to bed, and was being soothed by her mother and Mrs Spencer. Mary cried out, 'Oh Mrs Spencer, I did not throw her into the water. I took her into my arms and meant to die with her. I have heard people say that drowning is an easy death.' She continued by saying that she had been in the water for more than two hours, trying to drown herself after Adeline's death, but had been unable to do so.

It was now after one o'clock in the morning and Adeline's body was carried into the parlour. Another near neighbour, Matilda Wagstaff was called on to help, and she laid out the child's body. With Mrs Spencer, she went upstairs to help Mary undress and as the two women did so they found Mary's clothes to be extremely wet and filthy, suggesting that she had indeed been immersed in the mud and water of the pond. Mary's sister Alice opened a drawer to take out a nightdress, and found the letter Mary had written earlier that day, and which was addressed to her mother. In it she wrote that she had been abandoned once more by her seducer, and she ended the letter by saying that her family and friends would not see her again as she was intending to drown Adeline and herself.

A message was sent to Constable Hall, the local police officer, who arrived within a few minutes. On arrival he found Dr William Gregson examining Mary, who advised the officer that the young woman could be moved and taken to the lock-up if the constable so wished. However, Constable Hall was obviously a sensitive and understanding man, and he decided to let Mary get some sleep before having to face the ordeal that awaited her in the days ahead.

He sat by her bedside throughout the night, but Mary did not seem to be aware of his presence. She was restless and muttered a great deal to herself and repeatedly moaned that she wished she had saved Adeline. She also cried out, 'Oh my poor mother! Oh my poor child!' When she awoke the next morning, she was arrested and charged with her daughter's murder.

The inquest into Adeline's death took place on the following Tuesday at the Barley Mow Inn, Bonsall, before the area's deputy coroner, Mr Brookes. The court heard evidence from Mary's parents, Mr Spencer, whose wife was ill and could not attend, and Miss Wagstaff, all of whom described the events of Sunday night and the early hours of Monday morning. Constable Hall repeated what Mary had mumbled during the night and of her arrest the following morning on suspicion of murder.

Dr Gregson, who had performed a post-mortem on Adeline, gave details of his findings. There were no external signs of violence, although there was some slight discolouration to the side of the little girl's face, which he believed was a result of being held tightly against her mother's breast. The child's lungs were congested, but the rest of her organs were healthy. There were no signs of strangulation, and death was the result of being immersed in water. At the conclusion of the evidence the jury returned a verdict of 'found drowned'.

There was also a hearing before the magistrates at Matlock Bridge on Wednesday, 15 July, when a very pale Mary was brought into the dock. She showed no emotion as the witnesses were called to give their evidence, which was similar to that given at the inquest. However, Mrs Spencer had recovered and she was able to tell the court about the confession Mary had made to her. At the conclusion of the prosecution case, Mary's solicitor, Mr Skidmore, stated that he would not be calling any witnesses and that at the trial the defence would be relying on a plea of insanity.

The trial before Baron Huddleston took place at the Derby Assizes on Tuesday, 28 July, which was a little over three weeks since Adeline's death. None of the prosecution witnesses were challenged by the defence barrister Horace Smith, who set about convincing the jury that at the time Adeline was drowned, an act for which he acknowledged his client was responsible, Mary had been temporarily insane. He also emphasised that this had been no sham attempt at suicide by Mary. After holding her daughter under the water until she died, Mary had genuinely intended to drown herself, but despite being in the pond for over two hours, she had found it impossible to do so in just 3ft of water.

The Crown's medical witness, Dr Gregory, had examined Mary within two hours of the drowning, and he was of the opinion that she may have been suffering from brain fever, but he was not convinced she was insane at the time. However, the defence called Dr Webb, who had known Mary for many years, and he was firmly of the belief that she had not been sane at the time she drowned her daughter. He suggested that feelings of dejection or depression could indicate that insanity may possibly occur in an individual later. Those who did become insane frequently changed their disposition and might behave inappropriately towards those they loved best. Feelings of distress and anxiety, which Mary must have experienced on the Sunday morning she told her father about her second pregnancy, could accelerate any tendency towards insanity.

Other witnesses were called to give evidence on this issue. Elisabeth Spencer stated that as soon as she opened the door to Mary on the night of the killing, she had realised immediately that something was amiss and that the young woman seemed in very low spirits and was not in her right mind. Mary's father described his daughter as a devoted and loving mother who had until recently seemed very happy. However, in recent weeks she had become depressed and had taken to spending many hours alone in her room. She had always slept with Adeline in her bed, but her parents had become so concerned at this change in her personality that they arranged for their daughter Elizabeth to sleep in the room. Elizabeth described her sister as being bright and cheerful, who loved Adeline dearly. However, more recently she too had noticed her become withdrawn. Of course at this time none of the family knew the reason for her depression.

The defence was attempting to convince the jury that Mary had become dejected having realised she was pregnant once more, and this was exacerbated when her lover deserted her yet again. The unsympathetic response of her father had resulted in her becoming temporarily insane, which in turn led to her drowning Adeline, but failing to kill herself as she had genuinely wished to.

Even the prosecution was sympathetic, and in his final speech to the jury, Mr Weightman for the Crown said to them, 'It is a painful case and I would be glad if you could find a verdict in her favour, but you have your duty to do'. He pointed out that it was natural for a young woman in the accused's situation to become dejected, but there was no history of insanity, and he insisted that she had not been insane at the time she killed Adeline.

In his summing up, the judge told the jury that he acknowledged that as individuals he and they would no doubt wish to help any young woman who found herself in such distressing circumstances as the prisoner in the dock had done after first her lover abandoned her, and then her father told her she must leave the family home. However, he and they were concerned with justice on this occasion and he warned them, 'If you failed out of tenderness and weak-kneedness to do your duty, the time might come when the same thing will be turned against you in bitter reproach'. The jury heeded his words, for after deliberating for a little under thirty minutes they returned with a verdict of guilty to murder, but this was accompanied by a strong recommendation for mercy.

Baron Huddleston turned to Mary and said:

Prisoner at the bar, you have been convicted of the most serious offence known to the law. I quite agree with the verdict of the jury. In all probability you, overcome by the shame and dread of being turned out into the world, went into that mere. You wandered about irresolute for a long time, but ultimately entered the water with the intention of taking your own life and the child's too, and in the result you were saved, and the child was drowned. That in the eyes of the law is murder, but the jury have accompanied the verdict with the strongest recommendation for mercy, and that recommendation shall be forwarded to the proper officer of her Majesty, who I have no doubt will pay great respect to the recommendation of the jury, and to the circumstances of the case, and to the representation which I feel it to be my duty to make.

The only sentence available to the judge was the death penalty, and he asked Mary if she wished to say anything before it was passed. In a low, faltering voice Mary said simply that she was pregnant. English law forbade the execution of a pregnant woman, and in such cases the sentence was deferred until the condemned had given birth. In later years a doctor would examine the prisoner to confirm this, but in the 1880s, a jury of matrons was called upon to do so. Members of the court staff were no doubt prepared for Mary's statement, given the nature of the evidence heard during the trial. The High Sherrif was able to empanel twelve married women within a very short space of time.

Ly 117

At the Assizes and General delivery of the Gaol, holden at *Derby* —————— in and for the County of *Derby* —————— on *Tuesday* the twenty seventh day of *July* —————— in the forty fourth - year of the reign of our Sovereign Lady Victoria, by the Grace of God of the United Kingdom of Great Britain and Ireland Queen Defender of the Faith, and in the year of our Lord *1880*, before certain Justices of our said Lady the Queen assigned to deliver her Gaol of the said County of the Prisoners therein being

at *Derby*

Whereas at this present Session of Gaol Delivery

Mary Wright

is and stands Convicted of *Wilful Murder*

for which She is by Law, liable to suffer Death but Her Majesty having been graciously pleased to extend the Royal Mercy to her on condition of her being ~~Transported~~ Kept in penal servitude ~~beyond the seas~~; for the term of ten years, to be computed from the date of her conviction; and such intention of mercy having been signified to this Court in writing, by one of Her Majestys principal Secretaries of State, It is ordered, That the above named Convict be ~~Transported accordingly~~ Kept in penal servitude accordingly by the Court

Arthur D. Coleridge

Clerk of the Crown for the Midland Circuit

Confirmation of Mary Wright's reprieve. (National Archives)

4604 ✓

ORDER of LICENCE to a CONVICT
made under the Statutes 16 and 17
Vict., c. 99, s. 9, and 27 and 28 Vict.,
c. 47, s. 4.

2 MAR 1887

WHITEHALL,

28 day of *February* 1887

HER MAJESTY is graciously pleased to grant to

Mary Wright   who was

convicted of *Murder*

at the *Assizes holden at Derby*

~~for the~~

on the *27th* day of *July 1880*, and was then and there

sentenced to ~~be kept in Penal Servitude for the term of~~ *Death such sentence being afterwards commuted to Penal Servitude for a term of Ten Years*

and is now confined in the *Woking Female* Convict Prison,

HER ROYAL LICENCE to be at large from the day of her Liberation under this Order, during the remaining portion of her said term of Penal Servitude, unless the said

Mary Wright

shall,

before the expiration of the said term, be convicted of some indictable Offence within the United Kingdom, in which case such Licence will be immediately forfeited by Law, or unless it shall please Her Majesty sooner to revoke or alter such Licence.

This Licence is given subject to the Conditions endorsed upon the same, upon the breach of any of which it will be liable to be revoked, whether such breach is followed by a Conviction or not.

And Her Majesty hereby orders that the said

Mary Wright

be set at liberty within Thirty days from the date of this Order.

95783

Given under my Hand and Seal,

Mary Wright

LICENCE TO BE AT LARGE.

Henry Matthews

R & S (20,488a) 200 12—86

A copy of Mary Wright's licence. (National Archives)

The women went into a side room with Mary, and following their examination of her they confirmed that she was pregnant when they returned to the court. The judge thus directed that her execution should be postponed until after she had given birth to the child.

The case had understandably generated a great deal of interest throughout the county, and it emerged that public opinion was overwhelmingly sympathetic towards Mary. The *Derby Daily Telegraph and Reporter* came out strongly in her support, despite some misgivings regarding what it believed to be her loose behaviour. An editorial, in favour of a reprieve, stated that there was overwhelming evidence that she had been temporarily insane at the time of her daughter's death. The paper did not necessarily believe that her father's reaction to the news that she was pregnant for a second time was wrong, but it was felt that it did contribute to her state of mind at the time, as she was no doubt deeply worried about the prospect of being left unsupported with two children.

The author of one letter to the editor probably spoke for many. It read as follows:

Sir,

Mary Wright is condemned to be executed for the murder of her illegitimate child at Bonsall. The story of Mary's life is one of sad interest just now, and is fraught with many a warning for young men and for young women alike. There are cynical men who will say she ought to have known better. No doubt, but those who always do as they know are not inhabitants of a world like this. The anguish through which Mary passed before she could gather courage sufficient to take the idol of her heart – her little child – and place it in a cold pond, and walk into it herself with fond desire to take the dear babe with her into another world, can never by us be known. Far be it from me to justify murder, or law breaking of any kind. I only take up pen to plead for this girl's life, who cannot plead for herself, to say that she is deserving of mercy. Jesus Christ I think would – ah does – look with pity upon this lone woman in her sad plight. If ever a case fairly on its face bore traces of mental suffering and motherly love it is this one, and it requires no reproving words to bring home its lessons with awful force.

The law wisely provides that her Majesty may, if she so desire, remit the death punishment in a case like this. I appeal to our sisters, to men who have daughters, to do what they can to create and sustain a public sentiment in favour of a reprieve for this woman. There ought to be petitions, and I am sure they will be largely signed.

Truly yours,

W. Wilkinson.
3, Howard Street, New Normanton

Office 13169

PENAL RECORD.
(This Document is not to be folded.)

General Reg. No. in Convict Prisons. **G 117**

371/2

Name and Aliases Surnames	Christian Names	Reg. No. in County Prison	Sentence Years	Married or Single, and No. of Children	Name and Residence of Family or next of Kin.	Religion
Wright	Mary	131	Penal Servitude 10	Single	James Wright Bonsall Derbyshire	Protestant
		Age on Conviction Yrs. / Mon.	Police Supervn.			
		27 / o	None			

Crime (as given in Calendar)		Committal	Conviction	Trade or Occupation when free
Killing & Murdering one 'Adeline Wright' at Bonsall on the 4th July 80 "Wilful Murder"	Date	July, 9th 80	27 July 80	None
	Place	Matlock	Derby Assizes	

Character before Conviction and Information as to previous Convictions, if any.

Conduct	Good	Health	good	Education	Imp

Signature of Governor by whom the Prisoner is transferred to a Convict Prison. } C.E. Faynham

Description	On Reception into First Convict Prison	On Release from Convict Prison	Distinctive Marks or Peculiarities
Complexion	Fair	Pale	Scar left Knee
Hair	Light brown	Lt brown	Ears pierced
Eyes	Grey	Grey	
Height	4 feet 11½ Inches	4 feet 11½ in	
Build	Spare	Spare	
Shape of Face	Oval	Oval	

Name of Prison	Date of Reception			Name of Prison	Date of Reception			Trades or Occupations followed in Prison
	Day	M'th	Year		Day	M'th	Year	
Derby Millbank	20	9	80					Tailoring
Woking	18	3	81					
Licensed	28	3	84					

[For statement in reference to final disposal see next page.]

G117

Mary Wright's prison file. (National Archives)

Several petitions were signed by many thousands of people, and on 5 August 1880 Mary was informed by the governor of Derby Gaol that a reprieve had been granted, and her sentence commuted to one of ten years penal servitude. On her arrival in prison, medical tests confirmed that she had not been pregnant after all.

Initially she was sent to Millbank Penitentiary for a short time, before being transferred to Woking Female Prison, where she served seven years. She was released into the care of her father on 20 March 1887. One hopes she found some happiness in her life thereafter.

9

THE CHAMBER POT KILLING

Matlock Bridge, 1883

Twenty-two years after the conviction of George Smith for the callous and premeditated murder of his father, another parricide occurred in the county, but this case was of a wholly different nature.

George Marchant, a retired coachman, and his wife, Mary Ann rented out rooms to guests in their home, 'The Cottage' on Chesterfield Road, Matlock Bridge. On Tuesday, 27 February 1883, the Revd Julius Benn and his son, William Rutherford Benn, booked a suite of two adjoining bedrooms and a sitting room. The Revd Benn told the Marchants that he was hoping for a quiet and peaceful stay, which might be for just a few days or possibly for several weeks. He explained that his son was recovering from an illness and it was their intention to visit the town's renowned Smedley's Hydropathic establishment.

Sixty-year-old Julius Benn was a powerfully built man, measuring 6ft in height. He was a native of Manchester, and in his younger days had been a master at the Congregational Day School in Hyde, Cheshire. He later worked in London, where he remained for a number of years before taking a post in a boys' Reformatory School at Driffield in Huntingdonshire. He subsequently returned to London where for the previous fifteen years he had been the minister of the Old Gravel Lane Meeting House in Wapping. He was a well-known and highly respected figure in the capital's East End, where he was known for his efforts to improve the educational opportunities available to the youngsters of the poor in the area.

His son, twenty-eight-year-old William, was quiet and introspective. He was the third of his parents' seven children, and had been considering following his father into the ministry. He was intelligent, could speak

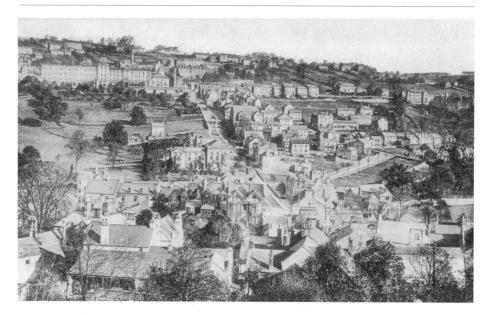

The Revd Julius Benn took his son William to Matlock Bridge to improve his health. (Author's collection)

The Benns enjoyed several long walks in the delightful Derbyshire countryside, and visited beauty spots including Millers Dale. (Author's collection)

The Benns also visited the Heights of Abraham. (Author's collection)

several languages, and until the end of 1882 he had been employed as a clerk in the City of London. He had been married in December of that year, to Florence Nicholson, but started to suffer from depression very soon afterwards. It had been hoped that taking time off work and resting at home would lead to an improvement in his health. However, his condition deteriorated to the extent that in January he was admitted into the Bethnal House Asylum, in which he remained for six weeks until 20 February. His condition had seemingly improved and he was discharged with a recommendation by asylum staff that he should continue his convalescence, and they suggested that an ideal place to do so would be the Matlocks in Derbyshire.

To the Marchants, the father and son seemed devoted to each other. Following their arrival they were in each other's company continuously, and took long walks together. On the Thursday they headed for Buxton and returned by way of Millers Dale, and on Friday they visited Riber Castle and explored the caverns.

On Saturday morning they walked to the Heights of Abraham and during the afternoon travelled by train to Comerford, from where they walked back through Matlock Bath. They returned to their lodgings in the early evening, and, after tea and having written several letters, the two men set off together for another walk. They returned at 9 p.m., and after William had taken his sleeping draught, as he had done every night since his arrival, the two men went to bed.

Matlock Bath was visited by father and son. (Author's collection)

At seven o'clock on the Sunday morning, the Marchants were woken by a loud banging noise. Initially they thought it was Mrs Marchant's mother, Mrs Julian, who lived with them. Mrs Marchant went to her mother's room to make sure she was all right, only to be told that her mother had not been responsible for the noise. Mrs Marchant returned to her room and stayed in bed for another hour, before getting up to prepare breakfast for her guests.

As the Benns had not come down for breakfast at their usual time of eight thirty, Mrs Marchant took a tray of food to their room. She knocked on their door but there was no reply, and she thought that they must have decided to sleep in until later as they were probably tired after the previous day's exertions. Furthermore, knowing that William took a nightly sleeping draught, she was reluctant to try and wake him up suddenly as she believed it was dangerous to do so.

The two men had not risen by midday, so their landlady took two cups of tea to their room, but there was still no reply when she knocked on the door, although she did hear a grunting sound coming from within the room. She waited for her husband to return from church one hour later, and told him of being unable to rouse their guests. He immediately went to the bedroom and after his repeated knocking on the door, opened it very slowly.

Standing in the doorway was William, who was wearing a nightshirt soaked in blood, and Mr Marchant also noticed that he had a deep wound to his throat. The young man did not speak but pointed towards the bed, on which his father, who had suffered a terrible head wound, was lying motionless. There was blood on the bed, the floor, all of the walls and the ceiling. A terrified Mr Marchant, fearing for his own life and that of his wife, rushed downstairs, grabbed her and ran out of the house to find help.

Within minutes, Dr Moxon and Dr Hunter arrived at the house, together with local police officers Sergeant Gee and Constable Smith. On reaching the bedroom, they found that the door had again been locked. However, when they called out to William, he opened it to them. Once inside the room, Dr Moxon said 'Good morning' to William, as he pushed him gently down into a chair, before tending to his throat wound, which he stitched and bound. He wrapped him in a blanket and he was then taken into an adjoining room by the police officers.

Given the extent of the wound to his head, it was obvious to the doctors that Julius was beyond medical help. There were no signs of a struggle, and they concluded that the fierce blows that had caused the damage must have been delivered while the victim was asleep. A search of the room revealed a large earthenware chamber pot under the bed, onto which blood and hairs from the victim were stuck: this was clearly the weapon used in the

Superintendent Sharpe travelled from Wirksworth to take charge of the murder investigation. (Author's collection)

assault. The search also led to the discovery of a penknife, which had blood on the handle and blade, and which had been used by William to inflict the wounds to his throat in an unsuccessful suicide attempt.

Later that afternoon, Superintendent Sharpe arrived from Wirksworth to assume responsibility for the investigation. His first act was to charge William with the murder of his father, to which he replied simply, 'Yes I did it'. Once he had been charged, William was taken to Derby Infirmary to receive treatment for the injuries to his throat.

The inquest into the victim's death opened at the Queen's Head at Matlock Bridge on the day after the discovery of his body. The body was formally identified by the nephew of the deceased, Charles Mycock of Hyde, and the hearing was adjourned until the following day to enable the remainder of the Benn family to travel north from London to be present at the hearing. It resumed as scheduled before Mr A.O. Brookes, Deputy Coroner for the High Peak District. William was not present at the hearing as he was still receiving treatment in the infirmary.

Following evidence given by the Marchants, the police officers who attended the crime scene, and details of William's confession to killing his father, Dr Moxon was called to the stand to give the medical evidence. He confirmed that the injuries to Julius were confined to the right side of the head, face and neck, and such was the force that had been used in inflicting the blows, that side of the head was completely shattered, and the right eye

Following his arrest, William Benn was taken to Derby Infirmary for treatment to his self-inflicted wounds. (Author's collection)

had been destroyed. He had found three wounds, the most serious of which had penetrated the skull, and this he believed had been caused by the chamber pot. There were two stab wounds to the upper and lower part of the ear, the lobe of which had been almost severed, and these injuries he determined had been caused by the penknife found at the scene. He concluded that the blow from the chamber pot had caused severe brain damage and had been the cause of death. He estimated that the victim had been dead for between five and six hours before his body had been discovered.

In answer to a question from a member of the jury, the deputy coroner confirmed that the inquest was not the appropriate tribunal at which to decide upon the state of mind of the accused man at the time his father had been killed. However, he assured the jury that it would be an important factor at his trial. It took the jury no time whatsoever to commit the accused to the next assizes, charged with wilful murder.

However, there would be no trial. William recovered from his physical injuries, but he was declared insane and was detained in an asylum under mental health legislation. Nevertheless, his family, including his wife Florence, remained supportive. In 1891, William's brother John, by then a leading politician, was advised by William's doctors that he had made a full recovery. John therefore approached the Home Secretary and gave his assurance that if William was released he would assume full personal responsibility for his brother's future behaviour.

The Home Secretary agreed to release him, and after being detained for eight years, William was released and returned to live with Florence in Balham, London. Twelve months later their daughter Margaret was born, but tragically there was to be no happy ending. Three years later Florence died and William's mental health again deteriorated badly. He was once again declared insane and was sent to Broadmoor, the asylum for the criminally insane, where he would spend the remainder of his life.

His daughter, Margaret, was raised by relatives and adopted the family name of Rutherford. At school she became interested in the theatre and decided upon an acting career. Margaret Rutherford made her West End debut in 1933 and became one of the country's leading and best-loved actresses. She appeared in many films and portrayed Agatha Christie's famous amateur detective, Miss Marple, in several, in which she solved a number of murders. She won an Oscar in 1963 and died in 1972.

10

MURDERED FOR THE INSURANCE MONEY

Swanwick, 1889

It was the afternoon of Tuesday, 28 May 1889, and miner George Horton was walking home, having finished his shift at the Alfreton Colliery a few minutes earlier. He was approached by PC Samuel James, who wasted no time in advising him that he was being arrested for the murder of Kate, his eight-year-old daughter, eight days earlier. The police had suspected Horton almost from the moment the girl's body had been discovered, but they had been waiting for the results of an analysis of her stomach contents before arresting him. These had now been received, and the police were certain they provided enough evidence to demonstrate that Kate had been deliberately poisoned by her father. He made no reply to the constable before being taken to Alfreton police station.

The alleged crime had taken place at the family home on Swanwick Lane, where Horton, whose wife had died nine months earlier, lived with five of his seven children. The two eldest girls were living away from home; Annie Elizabeth was in domestic service, and Rose Rachel was living with relatives in Lincolnshire, a decision which at the time Horton said had been made to ease the financial burden on the family following his wife's death. The Hortons lived in a relatively large house, which comprised two dwellings that had been knocked into one, and he had taken in lodgers to supplement his income. These were Mr and Mrs Browskill and their five children.

Downstairs, the scullery and living area were shared by both families, but upstairs, where each family had two bedrooms, there was a wall between them, which prevented any direct communication. On the

Swanwick, where George Horton lived with his family. (Author's collection)

Horton side of the wall, the father shared a bedroom with Kate and Joseph, and the other was shared by George, Charlotte and Sarah Jane.

Kate had always been a healthy and lively little girl, until the evening of Sunday, 19 May, when she returned from chapel with her family, and began to complain of stomach pains. She went to bed at seven o'clock and managed to sleep reasonably well. The following morning, at 5.30 a.m., Henry Browskill knocked on the adjoining bedroom wall as he usually did, to wake George Horton up in time for him to go to work. Sarah Jane, who was in the bedroom next to that of her father's, heard Kate ask him for a glass of water. She heard her father reply, 'I don't have enough time. If you want some water you will have to go downstairs and get it yourself.' This reply surprised Sarah Jane as Kate seemed to have been in a great deal of distress. A few minutes later she heard her father close the front door behind him as he left for the pit.

Sarah Jane and George were still in bed when a few minutes later Kate came into their bedroom. She was clearly in great pain and told her brother and sister that 'Daddy gave me something blue out of a bottle in a cup'. Sarah Jane carried Kate downstairs, and laid her down on the

The road leading from Swanwick to Alfreton, along which George Horton walked to work. (Author's collection)

sofa, while George went to fetch Mrs Browskill and another neighbour, Mrs Evans. By the time the two women arrived, Kate was barely conscious, but she did manage to tell the two women about the blue liquid she had been given by her father.

The youngster was suffering from acute stomach pains, her hands were tightly clenched, her legs were stiff, and her eyes and mouth twitched rapidly. Mrs Evans gave her a glass of water and sent for a doctor. However, Kate died twenty minutes later, before medical assistance arrived.

Henry Browskill rushed to Alfreton Colliery to inform Kate's father of the tragic news. However, when he arrived he was told that Horton had not turned up for work that morning. Henry waited for an hour at the pit gates, but as his neighbour did not arrive, he returned home to find that Horton was already there. He had come home unexpectedly at half-past eight to be told Kate had died. To those present at the scene he appeared to be genuinely distraught, and cried uncontrollably as he kissed the little girl's cheeks repeatedly. Sarah Jane mentioned that Kate had told them he had given her a blue liquid earlier that morning but he denied this most vehemently.

The morning his daughter died, her father walked into these fields rather than going to work. (Author's collection)

He insisted that he would not have gone to work if he had suspected Kate had been unwell, but when the police later learnt that he had not gone to the colliery that morning, it would fuel their suspicions of his responsibility for the little girl's death, as it suggested some foreknowledge on his part of what was about to occur. Frank Hall, one of Horton's workmates, told the police that he was walking towards the pit that morning, about 100 yards behind Horton, who, as he neared the gates to the colliery, unexpectedly left the main road and walked away from the pit and into a nearby field.

Horton was later seen in the fields by farmhand William Chapman who knew him well, and who recalled asking if he wanted to buy some food at the farm. Horton replied that he had simply decided to take a walk, adding, 'I may not see you for three or four days'.

Later that afternoon, young George returned home from school and was slapped across the face by his father, who had been told that his son had mentioned Kate's death to his school friends, and told them that his father had given her a mysterious blue drink shortly before she died.

The local coroner, Mr C.G. Busby opened the inquest the day following Kate's death, at the Boot and Slipper Inn, Swanwick, but immediately adjourned the hearing to allow a post-mortem to be performed by

Dr John Bingham of Alfreton. He also ordered that the dead girl's stomach contents should be sent to the district's analyst Mr A.H. Allen in Sheffield, to test for possible traces of poison.

Dr Bingham found no external injuries, which confirmed that she had not been subjected to any form of physical violence prior to death. He noted a brownish fluid, which he could not identify, had dribbled from her mouth, and although her organs showed no signs of damage, he found some blue particles in her stomach and small intestine. He put these organs in a sealed jar, which he forwarded to Mr Allen for analysis. The doctor could find no cause of death; that task would fall to Mr Allen.

The analyst discovered a number of worms, each 8 or 9in in length, in her intestines, but these were unrelated to her death. More significantly, he found evidence of strychnine in all her organs, which totalled eight tenths of a grain. He estimated that it would have taken one grain of the poison to kill a girl of her build and age, and he concluded that two grains had been administered. He also believed that it had been mixed with an ultramarine liquid, which had probably been a poison used to kill vermin. However, he could not identify the particular product used; those freely available at the time were Battle's, which was indigo in colour, Gabbitans's, which was white, and the pink-coloured Evison's. It was after he had forwarded this information to the police at Alfreton that Constable James was sent to arrest Horton.

At the adjourned inquest on 5 June, Mr Allen confirmed the results of his tests, and told the coroner that there was no doubt in his mind that strychnine had been used to poison the victim, and that she must have taken it about one hour before her death. The coroner's jury had no hesitation in finding Horton responsible for his daughter's murder, although as yet no motive for the crime had been identified.

The accused was born in 1852 and having experienced a better education than most of his contemporaries he was able to read and write to a high standard. Unfortunately he did not put this advantage in life to good use, for as a youth he had a reputation for laziness and dissolute behaviour. He was restless, unstable and found it difficult to hold down a job for very long.

His reputation did not improve greatly after his marriage and the birth of his children, for in those early days he was known to be a poor husband and father. Indeed, during the police investigation it emerged that Rose Rachel had decided to go and live with her relatives in Lincolnshire because of her father's regular violence towards her, and not to reduce the family's financial burden as he had claimed. He was out of work regularly and drank heavily. In 1884 the family moved from Newark to Swanwick, and it was only in the more recent past he had found employment at the colliery.

However, the illness and subsequent death of his wife appeared to have been a cathartic experience. He stopped drinking, joined the local Primitive Methodist Society, and he and his children began to attend the church regularly. Nevertheless, he found it difficult to cope financially, despite his two daughters leaving home and the extra rent from the Browskills. However, it did appear to those who knew him that he had adopted a more settled lifestyle and was taking his family responsibilities much more seriously. Sadly, this would prove not to have been the case.

The police discovered from John Wild, the Swanwick agent of the Refuge Insurance Company, that in the April of the previous year, Horton's late wife had insured the lives of all of the children, and paid one penny each week in respect of each of them. The agreement was that after paying for one year, the parents would receive £7 if Kate died, but had she died before April 1889 no payment would have been made on the policy. Thus, Kate's death was within a few weeks of her father becoming eligible for a payment of £7 upon her death, and this, the police believed, provided the motive for the little girl's murder.

There was at the time widespread concern regarding the link between insurance policies being taken out on children, and their subsequent murders by poverty-stricken parents. The Friendly Societies Act of 1846 had meant that insuring the lives of children under six years of age was forbidden, and that the insurance on children aged less than ten years was restricted to a maximum of £3. In 1855 however, these regulations were relaxed, meaning that children under five years of age could be insured for £6, and those aged between five and ten years could be insured for a maximum of £10.

Ostensibly, this meant that for a small weekly outlay to what became known as burial clubs, parents could ensure that in an age of high child mortality rates, especially among the poor, a decent burial could be provided for their children, thereby avoiding the shame of a pauper's grave. However, within a short time it was being claimed by some police officers, coroners, magistrates and judges across the country that many children were being murdered by their parents for the cash.

At the hearings of the Royal Commission on Friendly Societies in 1870, several witnesses had made such claims, but these went unheeded. In 1888, just one year before Kate's death, the Chairman of the Select Committee on Friendly Societies had stated that, 'The impression of our committee is that in fact, life assurance is a direct incentive to the destruction of infant life'. However, to the insurance companies this was a lucrative part of their business, for many thousands of weekly premiums of trifling sums of a penny or a halfpenny meant large amounts of cash. Such companies were powerful institutions, and successive governments drew back from confronting them over this issue. It was not until the twentieth century that legislation was introduced preventing the life of a child being insured.

In the Horton case the police believed that they had found evidence of premeditation when David Cowlishaw, another workmate of the accused, reported Horton having told him, 'I have got shut of two of the children, and should soon be shut of the lot, and then I'll take my hook'. Furthermore, the accused's daughter, Annie Elizabeth, told investigators that on one occasion, two months before Kate's death, she was being beaten by her father, who had screamed at her, 'I will poison you out of the road!'

Horton's trial took place at the Derby Assizes on 29 July 1889. He pleaded not guilty, and as he had been unable to afford a lawyer, the judge directed a barrister, Mr Appleton to represent him.

J.H. Etherington-Smith, who led the prosecution, acknowledged in his opening statement to the jury that the evidence against Horton was circumstantial. There was no scientific evidence which linked him directly to the crime, for nobody had seen him administer the poison, and the police had not been able to discover where the poison had been purchased by the accused. This was despite the determined efforts of Inspector Oldfield, who had personally visited all of the chemists for miles around Swanwick. The inspector had thought that Horton might have bought the poison at Ripley on the Saturday before Kate's death, when he had travelled there with the Browskills to visit the town's market. However, his neighbours assured the inspector he had not been out of their sight, and the officer failed to find any chemist in the town who remembered selling poison to anyone matching Horton's description. Nevertheless, Mr Etherington-Smith insisted that the Crown had established a motive and could prove that he made threats to rid himself of his children. There was also Kate's own statement that her father had given her the mysterious blue coloured drink shortly before she died.

Despite the very short notice at which he had accepted the brief, Mr Appleton was able to provide a spirited defence for his client. He emphasised the absence of an eyewitness and of physical evidence, together with the fact that there was no proof that poison had ever been present in the house, in which mousetraps had been used to catch vermin. Mr Appleton acknowledged that it was unlikely that anyone else in the house would have administered the poison, but he did suggest another scenario. Perhaps, he suggested to the jury, there was some poison in Kate's bedroom which nobody, including the deceased or her father, knew about, and she had taken it accidentally.

In his summing up to the jury, the judge also acknowledged the circumstantial nature of the evidence against the accused. He did however advise the jury that despite the sordid nature of the alleged motive, namely that Horton had murdered his daughter for £7 insurance money, they should not dismiss it as a possibility. After deliberating for thirty minutes the jury found him guilty, but before being sentenced to death, the condemned man insisted that he was innocent.

He continued to maintain his innocence until it became clear that there would be no reprieve. Now resigned to his fate, he made a full confession to Revd J.E. Matthews, vicar of Swanwick, who had visited Horton regularly in the condemned cell since his parishioner's conviction. He described buying the vermin killer he used to murder the girl, from the shop of chemist Mr Wain in Ripley some weeks prior to the crime, and using a false name when required to sign a poison register. After administering the poison, he had wandered in nearby fields before returning home. Although he had been teetotal for more than one year, he blamed alcohol for his continuing poverty and downfall. He had decided on murder, as he feared losing his home and the break-up of his family, which he had hoped the insurance money would prevent.

As his execution drew nearer, Horton wrote to his daughter Sarah Jane at the Belper workhouse, where the children were now living. The letter ended in the following way:

> God bless you all my Dear Daughter. You must be sure to pray to God to guide you all your life through and you must pray for your brothers and sisters. I do pray to God to guard you all your life through, so my Dear Daughter you must always think of what I have told you. You must always tell the truth and when you are tempted to do wrong you must pray to God for his help and he will hear you. Always remember that my Dear Children, and you must tell the others the same that is your brothers and sisters. God has promised to be a father to you always. Remember that he sees all that you do and all you think. Then if you do his will while here on earth he will receive you to his throne in glory where all is peace and rest. So my dear children you will be able to meet all your brothers and sisters and your poor dear mother in heaven, and by the help of God I shall meet you there too. So you must look to God for his help. You must never take anything that is not your own, and always tell the truth as I have always told you before.

Annie Elizabeth and Rachel Rose had already visited their father, knowing that he had confessed to the murder. He now asked Sarah Jane if she and the younger children would come to see him. The Belper Board of Guardians agreed that such a visit could take place, and the children arrived wearing their workhouse clothes. The warders, who were in the cell in which the visit took place, later described it as a harrowing experience.

The condemned man kissed his children repeatedly, and urged them not to take after him, but be honest throughout their lives. He wept as they left and remained inconsolable for several hours.

The prison authorities were becoming increasingly concerned as the execution date drew nearer. The last hanging at the gaol had been that of wife-killer Arthur Delaney, whose botched hanging resulted in his taking seven minutes to die as he was slowly strangled rather than dying instantaneously due to a broken neck, as he should have done. The governor, expressing his concerns and his desire to avoid a repetition of those unfortunate events, wrote to James Berry, who was to hang Horton. The experienced Berry replied, recommending that the iron beam from which the noose had been suspended for Delaney's execution be replaced by a wooden one, which the executioner believed would provide a certain amount of spring when the body fell, thus preventing a repeat of the earlier debacle.

Berry arrived the afternoon before the execution to find that the governor had followed his advice to the letter. He tested the scaffold and rope in order to ensure everything would proceed smoothly. Horton weighed 10st 4lb and was 5ft 3in tall. Berry initially calculated a drop of

*James Berry, whose professional expertise
ensured a trouble-free execution.*
(Author's collection)

5ft 6in, but after seeing that the condemned man was powerfully built and had a particularly strong and muscular neck, he extended the drop to 6ft.

On the morning of the execution, Wednesday, 21 August, Horton had to be roused by the warders at six o'clock. He went for a walk in the gaol's courtyard for twenty minutes, and on returning to his cell ate a breakfast of bread and butter and drank his final cup of tea. He was calm and appeared to have prepared himself for what lay ahead. At seven minutes to eight the chief warder entered the cell to accompany him to the scaffold, together with several other officials.

He had to walk across an open courtyard, and passed his own grave, which had recently been dug. Fortunately there were no problems at the execution and he died instantly of a broken neck, after which he was left suspended for one hour. The body was then cut down and the inquest opened at ten o'clock. Breaking with tradition, James Berry stayed behind to attend the hearing, and accompanied the jury to the place of execution where he explained how the drop had been calculated, and why he had recommended a wooden beam. A few minutes later, Horton was buried and this tragic case drew to a close.

11

THE ABORTIONIST

Osmaston, 1898

There were two murder trials at the Derby Winter Assizes of 1898, but the circumstances surrounding the crimes could not have been more different.

The first case concerned the death of Emily Eliza Robotham, a twenty-seven-year-old single woman, who in the autumn of that year realised that very soon she would be dead. Her health had deteriorated rapidly during the previous few days, and on Thursday, 7 September 1898, she explained what had caused her to be in such a poor condition to Dr Wheatcroft, who had been caring for her. Having listened to her account, the doctor hurriedly arranged for Emily to make a deposition on oath later that evening, in which she would repeat her account of the circumstances that had led to her imminent death.

Superintendent Airey was made aware that Emily had accused a Derby woman, Ruth Jane Talbot, a thirty-seven-year-old needlewoman of 66 Grayling Street, of being responsible. The superintendent called at the home of the accused woman to inform her of the allegations that had been made against her, and to request that she accompany him to hear the accusations directly from the mouth of her alleged victim. She and her husband travelled with Superintendent Airey to 17 Co-operative Buildings, Cotton Lane, Osmaston; the home of Mrs Coxon, with whom Emily had been staying.

There were several other people gathered in the bedroom in which Emily lay, including the dying woman's mother and several other relatives, Dr Wheatcroft, Mr A.B. Hamilton JP, who was to act as a witness to the deposition, and assistant magistrates' clerk H.R. Whitson, who was there

Osmaston Road. (Author's collection)

to write down the dying woman's words. The deathbed statement was brief, and in it Emily stated that on the previous Tuesday, Talbot had performed an abortion on her.

After the deposition had been made, Superintendent Airey arrested the accused woman for performing an illegal operation. She replied by asking, 'Shall I be allowed to go home tonight?' The answer was no, and Talbot was locked up in the local police cells. Two days later the superintendent informed her that Emily had died, and he charged her with murder. She burst into tears and the only words she uttered were, 'Oh, I am sorry'.

The tragedy had begun to unfold some weeks earlier. In July, Emily, who lived with her widowed mother and younger siblings in Abbey Street, Derby, told her mother that she was pregnant, and that the baby was due in late September or early October. Mrs Rowbotham made it clear to her daughter that she did not want the baby born in the family home. She cited lack of space but it is more likely that she did not wish the neighbours to know of the scandal that the family now faced.

Emily, however, was fortunate in one respect, for the putative father had promised not to abandon her, and had agreed to acknowledge the baby was his. Furthermore, he had promised Emily and their child financial support in the future.

Mrs Rowbotham became aware that Emily was in contact with Talbot, and was under the impression that she was simply a friend of her daughter's. However, Emily was discussing her immediate future plans with the other woman, but it is not known whether an abortion was being considered or discussed at this stage. Talbot recommended one address at which Emily might stay, but this was visited by her mother, who was not impressed, and this plan was abandoned. Mrs Rowbotham met Talbot, who was visiting her daughter, and the needlewoman said, 'I wish Emily was not so far gone, and I could have pulled her through. I have got many a one out of the same mess, but in her weak state I dare not touch her.'

Alarmed by this implicit threat of an abortion, which she had not realised was an option considered by her daughter, Mrs Rowbotham took matters into her own hands, and decided to make the necessary arrangements on behalf of Emily. She found her daughter accommodation with Mrs Coxon, where Emily was provided with her own comfortable bedroom. Mrs Coxon was a qualified and experienced midwife, and the arrangement seems to have been straightforward and legitimate, which involved Mrs Coxon arranging for proper medical care under the supervision of Dr Wheatcroft, who would also deliver the baby. The doctor visited his new patient regularly, and initially found her to be in good health.

Emily arrived on 20 July, and Talbot visited her after a few days and thereafter became a regular visitor. Emily's mother did not know of this, and Mrs Coxon presumed the two women were friends, and thought nothing more of it. However, by now Emily was facing a serious problem that needed to be resolved quickly. The man who had promised to support her financially, was in fact one of three men with whom she had been intimate earlier in the year. It was now realised that the baby was not that of the man supporting her, and if she was to convince him that it was his child she was carrying, it had to be born in August. If not, it would become obvious to him that the child was not his. Emily wanted their relationship to continue, and, worried that he may end it if he became aware that she had had another intimate relationship, she decided that she would have an abortion and paid Talbot £2 to perform it. This was with a view to telling the man afterwards that she had suffered a miscarriage. Later, Talbot would deny this, but did acknowledge that she had offered to perform an abortion with needles, but she insisted that Emily would not agree to such a course of action.

Dr Wheatcroft visited Emily on 24 August when she appeared to be in good health. Talbot visited her on the following day and again on 1 and 2 September. Two days later, assisted by Mrs Coxon, Emily gave birth to a baby who was stillborn. She told Dr Wheatcroft that it was a result of her falling downstairs when Mrs Coxon was out of the house two days earlier. However, he did not believe her account, for the baby's wasted state led the doctor to determine that it had been dead in the womb for at least two weeks.

On the following day, the doctor witnessed a rapid deterioration in his patient's condition, and her temperature rose to 106 degrees Fahrenheit. There was no improvement the following day and her temperature remained dangerously high. He realised that there was now no chance of her recovering, and told her the tragic news. It was then that she decided to inform the doctor of what had occurred, and told him that Talbot had used two needles to perform an abortion. The police were informed and arrangements made for her deathbed statement to be taken.

When Talbot was later advised that a post-mortem would be taking place, she replied that she felt easier in her own mind as this would demonstrate that nothing unlawful had occurred. This, however, seemed to be bravado on her part. The examination was performed by Dr Wheatcroft and Dr Spettigue. They found indications of blood poisoning and two perforations, which they insisted was conclusive evidence of instruments such as needles being used, which supported Emily's version of events. The cause of death was acute septic poisoning, arising from an illegal operation as described by the deceased.

The inquest into Emily's death opened on Thursday, 16 September before Mr A. Taylor, Deputy Coroner for Osmaston. This however, was only a brief hearing and was restricted to evidence of identification of the deceased so that a burial certificate could be issued. The hearing was adjourned until the following Wednesday at the Sherwood Foresters Hotel, Old Normanton. It was at this hearing that the coroner's jury, having heard all of the evidence, found that the dead woman had been the victim of wilful murder by Talbot, and furthermore it was considered there had been no accessories to the crime.

Talbot also appeared before a special sitting of the County Bench at the County Hall, Derby, at which evidence similar to that given at the inquest was heard. The magistrates also committed her to the next assizes for trial.

Her trial took place in early December, with the prosecution being led by J.H. Etherington-Smith, who was assisted by Mr Garratt. The accused was defended by W.B. Hexall.

Mr Etherington-Smith opened the prosecution case by describing the crime as a murder in the second degree. It was acknowledged that the defendant had not intended to kill Emily, but the crucial element of malice aforethought, necessary in all cases of wilful murder, was understood to be present in law in such cases. He next called the witnesses for the prosecution, all of whom had testified at the inquest and before the magistrates. The evidence that each gave at the trial was similar to that which had been given at those previous hearings.

In his concluding address to the jury, Mr Etherington-Smith emphasised the importance of Emily's deathbed statement. He accepted fully that she had colluded in arranging the abortion, but this did not remove the responsibility of the accused for what occurred.

In Talbot's defence, Mr Hexall insisted that his client had simply made an internal examination of the deceased. However, he insisted that the internal injuries that had undoubtedly caused Emily's death were not the result of an attempt to perform an abortion, but by Talbot's failure to perform a proper and safe examination. He urged the jury to return a verdict of manslaughter, which he claimed was the most appropriate outcome in this sad case.

In his summing up, the judge very fairly acknowledged that an abortion that went horribly wrong and ended in the death of the pregnant woman, was not the usual type of murder that juries had to decide on. Paradoxically, the victim of such crimes had often solicited the illegal operation. Nevertheless, he continued by making it clear that if an individual commits a felonious act which could reasonably be foreseen to endanger the life of another, and death results, that individual is guilty of murder.

He told the jury that they had to decide whether they believed that the accused woman had performed the illegal operation knowing that it might possibly end Emily's life. He drew their attention to the accused's suggestion to the deceased's mother that it had been regrettable that Emily had not approached her earlier, as she would have been able to help her without risk. The jury might reasonably conclude that this demonstrated an awareness that Emily's life would be at risk if an abortion was attempted.

If they did believe this was the case, the fact that Talbot had not intended to harm her was not an issue in determining guilt or innocence. As for the defence claim that their client had not performed an operation as such, but had simply carried out an internal examination, the judge pointed to the post-mortem findings and suggested that the members of the jury might believe this cast serious doubt on that explanation.

The jury retired at 6.35 p.m. and returned twelve minutes later having reached their verdict. The foreman stated, 'We find the prisoner guilty of wilful murder, but with a strong recommendation for mercy, seeing that she was sent for and did not seek the opportunity herself.'

The judge replied, 'I shall have pleasure in forwarding your recommendation to the Home Secretary, and I have no doubt it will receive at his hands the most careful consideration.' He passed the mandatory sentence of death, and the prisoner, who appeared stunned by the verdict, had to be helped by the prison warders down the steps into the cells below.

The jury's recommendation for mercy, which obviously had the support of the judge, did not necessarily mean that a reprieve was inevitable. Abortionists had been hanged occasionally when their operations had gone wrong and ended in the death of a pregnant woman. Accordingly, Talbot's solicitor, Mr Holbrook wasted no time in raising a petition in the hope of gaining his client a reprieve.

On 7 December, Sir George Sitwell, the High Sheriff of Derbyshire, received a letter from the Home Office confirming that Talbot had been reprieved, and when this news was conveyed to her in the condemned cell at Derby Gaol, she collapsed.

It was to be another two weeks before she was advised of the sentence she would have to serve, when, on 23 December, Mr Holbrook received notification from the Home Office that she was to be sentenced to twelve years' penal servitude. However, if during her sentence she was industrious and well behaved, she would become eligible for release on licence after eight years.

12

THE BRUTE

Bugsworth, 1898

The second murder trial at the winter assizes of 1898 was that of seventy-one-year-old John Cotton. He had spent his working life as a boatman, and had a reputation for extremely violent behaviour against women. His long-suffering wife, Hannah, who was thirty-five years his junior, and who lived with him in the cramped conditions of their barge, was frequently the victim of his brutal outbursts. He would become intensely jealous if Hannah so much as looked at another man, and he regularly accused her of having affairs, even though she was known to be a faithful and dutiful wife.

On Wednesday, 26 October 1898, their barge was moored in the Upper Peak Forest Canal's terminus at Bugsworth, near Whaley Bridge, and that afternoon the couple decided to go for a drink at the Rose and Crown. The Cottons were well known to the landlord, Thomas Hayes and his wife, as they visited the pub whenever they moored in the basin.

As the afternoon wore on, Cotton began arguing with his wife and became extremely threatening. The landlord attempted to placate him, and eventually persuaded Cotton to take Hannah home. Worried what Cotton might do to her, Thomas walked with the couple to where their boat was moored, by which time Cotton appeared to have calmed down. When Thomas left them Cotton appeared to be on good terms with his wife. Little could he know that Hannah would soon become the victim of a murderous attack by her husband.

As soon as they were back on the barge, Cotton started to abuse his wife. Gradually his anger increased to such an extent that he picked up a poker, 3ft in length and 1in thick, with which he began to beat her.

The Upper Peak Forest Canal, on which Cotton made his living. (Author's collection)

Bugswort Basin. (Author's collection)

This was witnessed through an open cabin door by three young girls who were on their way home from school.

Elizabeth Copeland, Selina Hall and Hilda Hayes were on the opposite canal bank when they heard Hannah's screams coming from the boat. The girls looked on in horror as Cotton savagely beat his unfortunate victim repeatedly about the head with the poker. After a number of blows Hannah fell silent.

The crime was also witnessed by local farmer, James Carrington, whose evidence would later suggest that this was not simply a drunken and unpremeditated assault on Hannah. Rather it seemed to him to have been a deliberate and calculated attack, a view which was given additional support by the landlord of the Rose and Crown, who testified that in his opinion, Cotton had not been drunk when he left the pub earlier that day.

James Carrington also heard Cotton shouting at Hannah as he continued to beat her. As she lay helpless on the cabin floor, pleading for mercy, he could hear her attacker mocking her, and screaming that if she did not shut up he would throw her into the canal. He also shouted that he was tired of her and wanted rid of her so that he could find a new wife.

Cotton left the boat, and after he did so, Mr Carrington and the three girls took the opportunity of calling for help. Hannah was carried to the nearby Navigation Inn, where she was treated by Dr Allen. Cotton meanwhile had returned to the Rose and Crown, where for the next few hours he drank heavily. By this time news of his vicious attack on Hannah had spread and the landlady said to him, 'You've done it this time Cotton'. His response was to say to her, 'If you don't hold your tongue, I'll serve you the same as I've served her'. At this stage neither of them was aware of the true extent of Hannah's injuries, but later that night he was arrested by Constable Whitely, who had recovered the weapon used in the assault, for the attempted murder of his wife.

However, Hannah died the following morning without having regained consciousness, and the charge was therefore amended to that of wilful murder. The brutal nature of the assault was revealed when the post-mortem was performed by Dr Allen of Whaley Bridge and Dr Anderson of Chapel-en-le-Frith. The victim's head was a mass of severe cuts and large bruises. One of the blows had fractured the base of her skull, and this alone was described as having been sufficient to have caused her death.

The inquest was held on the following Saturday morning before local coroner Mr G. Davis. The coroner's jury had little difficulty in finding that Hannah had been the victim of wilful murder and that her husband was responsible. On the following Thursday Cotton appeared before the Magistrates' Court at Chapel-en-le-Frith Town Hall. Once again this proved to be little more than a formality, and despite his attempt to interrupt the evidence being given by Elizabeth Copeland by calling her a liar, Cotton was committed to stand trial at the next assizes.

The Navigation Inn. (Author's collection)

As Cotton, who had been remanded to Derby Gaol, awaited his trial, details of his background began to emerge. He had made relatively few previous court appearances, and these had been mainly for drunkenness and minor offences. Surprisingly, there had been no convictions for violence. This was, however, probably due to the fact that hitherto his victims had been too frightened to report him to the police.

In the past he had been heard to boast that he had killed his two previous wives, which was a claim he appeared to take a good deal of perverse pride in. These deaths had not been due to one attack, but rather to his continuing ill treatment of them over lengthy periods of time. Someone who had known him for many years told a local reporter of one occasion when he threw his wife out into the street after beating her very badly, and on another occasion he injured the same woman so badly that when suckling her baby it had to be held to her breast by a neighbour.

At his trial, Cotton's defence barrister, Mr Lawrence, argued that the jury should convict his client of manslaughter, as there had been no intent to kill his wife. However, this argument was rejected and at the trial's conclusion the jury took just fifteen minutes to return a verdict of guilty of murder. Ominously for Cotton, there was no recommendation for mercy.

The trial judge, Justice J.C. Mathew, expressed his full agreement with the jury's verdict. He exhorted Cotton to make the most of the short time he had left to prepare himself for his death, and to repent, after which he sentenced him to death.

The brutality of the crime, the lack of a recommendation for mercy, together with the public's obvious indifference to the callous murderer's fate, meant that there would be no petition to obtain a reprieve. It was thought that the Home Secretary might intervene to prevent his execution due to Cotton's advanced age. However, there was to be no such intervention, and the execution was fixed for 21 December.

In the condemned cell, Cotton was visited daily by the prison chaplain, the Revd J. Hart-Johnson, who reported that the prisoner had demonstrated what he considered to be genuine repentance. On the eve of his execution Cotton was visited by his two sons and one of his daughters for the final time. The visit was brief but intensely emotional, and he told them that he believed he had been granted a heavenly pardon. He lay on his bed at 9 p.m., but was unable to sleep and spent a restless night.

The hangman James Billington and his son, William, had arrived at the prison during the afternoon prior to the execution, and made all the necessary preparations for the following morning. The scaffold was relatively new and had been used on just one previous occasion in 1896. A huge crossbeam had been built into the walls of the execution chamber, 8ft from the ground, to which the Billingtons fixed the rope. The lever was tested and found to be in good working order.

Cotton was out of bed and dressed by 5.30 a.m. and enjoyed a traditional last breakfast of bread and butter with a cup of tea. At 7 a.m. the prison chaplain entered the cell to offer some comfort to the condemned man. The governor allowed five journalists to be present at the execution, and they were met at the gate by the gaol's schoolmaster, Mr W. Fenwick who escorted them the forty yards to the place of execution. *En route*, the journalists had to pass a newly dug grave immediately under the main wall, which within a few hours would be Cotton's final resting place.

Shortly before eight o'clock the county sheriff and the other officials arrived at the door of the condemned cell. Cotton was advised that the time for his execution had arrived, and the procession made its way to the scaffold. At its head was Chief Warder Lawrence, who carried a black wand. Cotton followed immediately behind him, and walking alongside him were Warders Evans and Langdon. Warders Cox and Sills followed, and at the rear of the procession were the governor, Captain C.E. Farquarson, the acting Under Sheriff Mr H. Scott-Currey, and finally the prison surgeon, Dr C.A. Greaves.

The chaplain joined them on the scaffold, and he was reading from the English Burial Service as Cotton, whose hair was noticeably whiter than at his trial, climbed the steps. He stood on the trapdoor calmly as Billington's son fastened the ankle strap, and Billington senior placed the noose around his neck and made the necessary adjustments. Finally a white cap was placed over his head, and the bolt was drawn. As Cotton plunged through the trap the chaplain was saying, 'Oh Lord remember not the offences of Thy servant', to which the others in the room responded, 'Amen'.

The execution took place on the shortest day of the year, and although it was a cold and dark morning, a large crowd had gathered outside of the prison walls. There was no sympathy for Cotton, and his execution seems to have been welcomed by the assembled crowd. Two policemen were present, but the crowd was well behaved and posed no problems. As the prison clock struck eight o'clock all eyes turned towards the flagstaff to watch the black flag raised to confirm the execution had taken place. The crowd then dispersed quietly.

Two hours later the inquest was held before the coroner, Mr W. Harvey-Whiston, and the jury found that he had been hanged lawfully. Within a few minutes, the body of this violent and unlamented man was placed in the freshly dug grave under the prison wall.

13

A MATRICIDE

Chesterfield, 1905

Throughout the twentieth century just seven men were executed in England for the particularly heinous crime of murdering their mothers, and two of these matricides occurred in Derbyshire. The first took place in Chesterfield in the early years of the century.

It was a few minutes before ten o'clock on the morning of Sunday, 6 August 1905 when Henry Dye, who was delivering newspapers, approached the door of 3 Spa Street, Chesterfield. He found the door open and peering into the house, he was horrified to see the body of fifty-one-year-old Mary Fallon lying on the floor.

Henry found Constable Sykes, who returned to the house with the distressed witness. Once at the scene, the officer found the body to be cold and stiff, suggesting she had been dead for several hours. He also noticed that the room in which she lay showed signs of a desperate struggle. He knew that the victim had been disabled and could only walk with the aid of a crutch. This, together with much of the furniture in the room, was broken and there was a great deal of smashed crockery and glassware. The crutch and a chair leg were lying close to the body, and were covered with blood.

It was obvious to Constable Sykes that death had not been due to an accident, natural causes or suicide, and that he was standing at the centre of a murder scene. He made an initial search and in an upstairs bedroom he found the deceased's twenty-nine-year-old son, John Silk, asleep in his bed. He was wearing a blood-soaked shirt and trousers, and there were bloodstains on both of his hands.

Gent. Mag. Dec.r 1819. Pl. II. P. 497.

SOUTH VIEW OF CHESTERFIELD CHURCH, DERBYSHIRE.

Chesterfield was the setting for a brutal matricide in the early years of the twentieth century. (Derby local Studies Library)

The officer shook the sleeping man vigorously, until he eventually woke up. Silk seemed genuinely surprised and distraught when advised of his mother's death, but he was arrested on the spot on suspicion of being responsible. The two men went downstairs, and as they did so, the prisoner walked over towards the sink to wash the blood from his hands, but he was prevented from doing so by the officer.

The police surgeon, Dr W.J. Symes arrived within minutes of the body being discovered. He was able to confirm that she had been killed on Saturday night. Externally, he discovered serious injuries to her head, face and throat, and her hair was matted with blood. There was a large bruise to the right side of her head, her right eye was badly damaged, there were large bruises to her left cheek and jaw, her nose was broken and her throat was bruised. There were extensive injuries to her right breast, right shin, and her left arm was bruised and badly cut.

Later that afternoon Dr Symes performed a post-mortem. He found five broken ribs, the ends of which had been driven into her lungs, which as a result had been badly damaged. The external injuries together with the nature and extent of the internal damage had, Dr Symes concluded, resulted from great force being used by her assailant, who had probably jumped on her as she lay on the floor. Death was due to shock arising from the cumulative effects of her multiple injuries.

Silk claimed to have no memory of the events of the previous night, but the police had little difficulty in finding several witnesses whose statements pointed to him as having been responsible for the crime.

On the morning of the murder Silk had gone to work as usual and he arrived home at 1 p.m. He changed into his best clothes before visiting several local pubs. He was soon drunk and returned home a number of times during the late afternoon and early evening.

Ruth Allsop lived next door to the Silk family, and she saw him in the house at eight o'clock in the evening, when she heard mother and son arguing. She heard him return two hours later, and from her window, Ruth saw his mother hand him a bottle, and ask him to fetch her half a noggin of whisky. He was drunk and refused her request, and grabbed the bottle from her hand before smashing it. He picked up several pieces of glass and threw them into her face, causing a number of cuts.

Silk left the house and Ruth saw him meet his friends Daniel Meakin and Arthur Watson, with whom he continued drinking. His friends later told the police that in one pub they sat next to a courting couple, and Silk began flirting with the young woman. At first her companion did not seem too concerned, but Silk persisted in forcing his attention on her, and eventually the young man took exception to Silk's behaviour and the two men began to quarrel. It seemed likely that a fight would follow, and as the argument continued, all five were ordered to leave the premises by the landlord.

Silk would not let the matter drop and was determined to fight the other man on the pavement outside the pub. However, he was restrained by his friends, and the other man left the scene with his girlfriend. In his drunken rage, Silk screamed, 'By Christ, there'll be a murder in Spa Lane tonight!' His friends tried unsuccessfully to calm him down, but he continued to struggle with them, and at last shouted, 'It will be our old girl!' His friends presumed this was the alcohol talking, and did not realise that this would prove to be more than an idle threat.

Silk arrived home later to find his mother and their lodger Thomas Meakin sat at the table. Still drunk and quarrelsome, Silk complained to his mother about the poor light provided by the single gas lamp in the centre of the table. He leant over to turn up the flame, but his mother told him not to do so. Silk became even angrier and hit her on each side of her head with his open hand. Following this, he punched her to the floor, and in doing so knocked the table over and extinguished the lamp, leaving the room in darkness. Nevertheless, Thomas could hear the terrible beating continue, and heard the poor woman scream out, 'Murder!'

Thomas ran from the house in search of a police officer, and came upon Sergeant Prince. He informed the officer of what was happening, but the sergeant, who knew the Silks, refused to intervene, saying that this was nothing unusual when mother and son were drunk, and the argument would soon come to an end. Thomas returned to the house alone, and found it to be quiet and in darkness. He tried to gain entry but was unable to do so as the door was locked. Believing the argument had ended as the sergeant had predicted, Thomas went to a friend's house where he spent the night. However, neighbours Emma Watson and Nelly Goodwin both later told the police that they had heard the sounds of a terrible argument and struggle resume later that night.

Following the discovery of the body, Thomas briefly came under suspicion by some of the investigating police officers, due to what they claimed to be a significant inconsistency in his account. This was his claim to have found the door to the house locked, whereas Henry Dye had found it open a few hours later. However, he was quickly dismissed as a suspect, and how the door came to be open was to remain a mystery.

Silk was committed to stand trial at the next assizes by the local magistrates and on a coroner's warrant following a committal hearing and an inquest. At both tribunals he was found to have been responsible for his mother's murder. The trial took place on 8 December and the judge was Mr Justice Bucknill. The Crown was represented by J.H. Etherington-Smith and the accused's counsel was Dominic Daly.

John Silk was the victim's son from her first marriage, and he had served in the 5th Lancers for eight years with great distinction, before being honourably discharged from the Army in 1903. Prior to that he had served in India and in South Africa, where he saw action in the Boer War. In India he had suffered a lengthy and debilitating bout of enteritis, and while serving in Africa he had experienced a serious fever which had resulted in his weight dropping from thirteen stone to just seven.

At the time of his discharge his mother had recently separated from her third husband, and it seemed logical that he, a single man, should live with her. Generally they lived together on good terms, and he gave her most of his wages. However, his dependence on alcohol had increased, and in tandem with this so did the level of his violence against her, which was described to the jury by two of his close relatives, John Canavan and Micheal O'Brien. They also described instances of bizarre behaviour by the accused when drunk. He would run through the streets yelling at the top of his voice, apparently believing that he was back in South Africa fighting the Boers.

Both witnesses also confirmed that Mary had suffered from a serious drink problem, which had exacerbated the problems at home, as she too could be quarrelsome and aggressive when under the influence of alcohol. Michael told the court that he had seen Mary on the night of the murder and confirmed that she had been drunk. The defence also called a character witness, Henry Cain of the Chesterfield Board of Guardians, who had known Silk since his childhood. He told the court that before joining the Army he had been a 'very good lad', but following his discharge, his mental health had seemed to deteriorate badly. However, the defence did not call an expert witness to attempt to prove Silk had been insane, and appeared to be simply attempting to elicit some sympathy from the jury for their client.

The prosecution, however, had little sympathy for the accused, and when addressing the jury, Mr Etherington-Smith said:

> I fail to see what could be advanced from the evidence to reduce the charge from anything but murder. If it were an excuse that because he had had enteritis in India and fever in South Africa, he was weakened by drink, and therefore not responsible for his actions, human life would not be safe.

Mr Daly did not attempt to persuade the jury that Silk was not responsible for his mother's death when he addressed them. He suggested rather that manslaughter was the appropriate crime he should be convicted of, as there had been no malice aforethought, and there was no evidence that he had borne his mother any ill will. However, in his summing up, the judge made it clear that he was not impressed by the defence argument. He reminded the jury that there had been no evidence provided to support the claim that the accused did not fully know what he was doing, or what the consequences of his actions would be.

John Ellis, seen here demonstrating his skills as a hangman, assisted in the execution of John Silk. (Rochdale Local History Library)

After retiring for fifteen minutes the jury returned with a guilty verdict. In sentencing him to death the judge told Silk, 'The jury has found you guilty of taking the life of your mother under exceptionally brutal circumstances. I can hold out no hope of mercy for you in this world. She got no mercy from you, nor shall you get any from man.'

Despite the judge's suggestion that there was little hope of avoiding the noose, a number of his friends and relatives organised a petition. However, it received hardly any support from the wider public, and it soon became clear that he would inevitably hang for his crime. Nevertheless, he continued to receive much support from his family members who visited him regularly in the condemned cell at Derby Gaol.

He also corresponded with family and friends, and he sent this moving letter to his grandmother:

Dear Grandmother,

I have received your letter all right, and I write in return to let you know that I am all right and keeping well in health, thank God for it. I am sorry to hear that you are ill, and I hope that this will find you better, and that God will spare you to your family for some considerable time. I pray you do not let your heart grieve too much in this your great trouble, but rather hope that it is all for the best, and that God in His infinite mercy will help us to bear it patiently and bravely for His sake. I am happy to be able to inform you that I have received the Blessed Sacrament this morning, and feel a great peace in my heart. You know how we feel, or perhaps how we ought to after having attended to this great duty, and I think you will be cheered up by the knowledge of it. I hope Uncle John is all right, and I have to thank him for his kindness to me and I hope he will be rewarded for it in the time to come. I wish you would let me know which of you and how many wish to come and see me, so that I can let the governor know definitely how many to send permits for. You can't all come at once. I think so many come at a time would be best. I don't think I need say a deal more at present except to send you all my best love and heartiest good wishes. I remain your affectionate grandson.

John

Nevertheless, as his execution drew nearer, Silk decided not to see any of his family, in the hope of saving them from any further distress than necessary. On the final family visit he assured his relatives that he would die like a soldier.

The condemned's execution, which was to be carried out by Thomas Pierrepoint assisted by John Ellis was set for 8 o'clock on the morning of Friday, 29 December 1905. The four journalists who gathered at the scene on a cold wet and misty morning later confirmed that he did indeed die bravely.

A crowd of several hundred waited outside the gates of the gaol, waiting for the black flag to be raised confirming that the execution had taken place. However, they waited in vain as the governor had decided to dispense with this morbid custom.

14

THE DISAPPEARANCES

Glossop, 1923

T homas Wood, who lived at his family home, 96 Back Kershaw Street, Glossop, was not quite four years old, but he was allowed to play out on his own by his parents. They were not unduly worried therefore when he ran out of the house on the morning of Sunday, 4 March 1923. He did not come home for his lunch, but he often ate at his grandmother's house, which was nearby. However, he had not returned by the early evening, and his parents learnt from his grandmother that he had not visited her that day.

Now deeply worried, his parents alerted the police and a search was begun immediately. As news of his disappearance spread throughout the close-knit community, it was not long before many volunteers offered their services to look for the missing youngster. Albert Burrows, who lived next door to the Woods at no. 94, reported seeing the boy that afternoon on Slatelands Road. This was a cause of some concern, for a stream ran alongside a stretch of that road which came down from the hills and eventually joined the River Etherow. For some days, the stream had been a fast flowing torrent due to a combination of recent heavy rains and the melting of a large amount of snow that had fallen two weeks earlier.

It was feared that Tommy may have fallen into the stream and been swept away, for he would have had very little chance of survival. The search centred on the stream and river for the next few days, and they were dragged repeatedly. A local resident loaned his bloodhound to help

The Nab. (Author's collection)

in the search, but no trace of Tommy was found. Given the lack of success in finding the boy, it was decided to widen the search.

The police received new information suggesting that Tommy had been seen close to two disused mine shafts which were situated about a half mile from Simmondley on the Charlesworth Road at the foot of a hill, known locally as the Nab. It was feared that he might have fallen down one of them, for despite the dangers, access was relatively easy. Also it would not have been difficult for anyone who had harmed the youngster, to throw him into one of the shafts. On Monday, 12 March, a grappling iron was thrown down one of the shafts, but the rope snapped and it was decided to make another attempt the following morning.

Inspector Chadwick, who was responsible for the search, passed the other disused shaft, the wall surrounding which was 6ft in height. He noticed that in one spot, about 2ft from the ground, a number of bricks had been removed, and the hole was large enough for someone to crawl through. He was with Herbert Collier, one of the volunteers who knew the area well, and he confirmed that the breach in the wall had appeared within the last fortnight. The inspector decided that on the following day, he would start by investigating that shaft.

The next morning, the grappling iron was cast down into the shaft and immediately fastened onto an object. This was raised but it was found to be a container full of stones. The iron was thrown down for a second time, and very quickly attached itself to something else. This was raised very carefully and on reaching the surface it could be seen that at the rope's end, caught on the iron by the trousers, was the body of a little boy. This was witnessed by a large crowd of spectators who had gathered at the site, and among them was Tommy's uncle who identified the body as that of his nephew.

This was now a murder enquiry and suspicion fell on Albert Burrows, who had often taken Tommy for walks with the agreement of his parents. Initially he told police that he had not taken him out walking on the day he disappeared. However, several witnesses, including Samuel Robinson and Jane Sidebotham, reported seeing Burrows with a young boy, to whom he gave an apple, on the morning of Tommy's disappearance. Although none of these could say definitely that the boy was Tommy, it certainly served to increase the police interest in Burrows. This was especially so when another witness, Fred Burgess remembered seeing Burrows with a boy earlier in the day, and walking back into town later, on his own from the direction of Simmondley. John Pale reported that he too had met Burrows that afternoon, who said, 'If you see Tommy Wood, send him home, he's lost'.

When the police confronted him with this information, Burrows changed his story and admitted that he had taken the youngster for a walk to the fields at Simmondley, close to the two disused pit shafts. There, Burrows insisted that he had left Tommy in a hollow while he went to catch a rabbit. When Burrows returned to the spot fifteen minutes later, Tommy had disappeared. This did not satisfy Inspector Chadwick who believed that Burrows knew more than he was prepared to admit, and he ordered that his movements be watched.

Burrows was under police surveillance at the time that Tommy's body was removed from the shaft, and the inspector knew he was watching from a distance despite attempting to hide himself from view. When he saw Tommy's body being laid out on the ground, Burrows began to hurry away from the scene, and the inspector ordered his men to detain him. A section of the crowd noticed what was happening and they also began to chase Burrows who was now running as fast as he could.

The following day's newspaper reports described Burrows being apprehended by a group of local men, who handed him over to the police, when the officers arrived at the scene several minutes later. However, there was a determined attempt to hang Burrows from a nearby tree, and if the police had arrived any later he may well have been lynched. Burrows reportedly told his captors, 'I don't know what made me do it' and pleaded for mercy. One of the crowd retorted, 'You didn't show much mercy to little Tommy'.

Now in handcuffs, Burrows was taken to Glossop in an open lorry, and a large number of angry local people lined the route and shouted abuse and threats at him. Others threw objects at him, and in response, he shook his fists at his tormentors and referring to the notorious Victorian murderer, shouted, 'I shan't tremble on the scaffold like Charlie Peace!'

Despite being arrested, Burrows was not immediately charged with Tommy's murder. During the following two weeks, he made several appearances before the local magistrates and also before Mr G.H. Wilson, the Deputy Coroner of the High Peak District. Whenever he appeared he was confronted by a large and hostile crowd, and on every occasion he continued to be abused and have missiles thrown at him. There were real fears as to what might happen to him on these occasions, and the police had to resort to decoy vehicles to ensure his safety as he travelled between Strangeways Prison in Manchester, where he was being held, and the hearings in Glossop.

Dr J.H. Dible, Professor of Pathology at Manchester University performed a post-mortem on Tommy on 15 March, at which he was accompanied by the local police surgeon, Dr E. Milligan. Tommy was found to have been a well-nourished and healthy youngster before his death. The soddened condition of his skin confirmed that he had been immersed in water for several days prior to the body being discovered. Dr Dible found several external injuries, which had been caused before death. No bones had been broken, but there were bruises on his left shoulder, on the underside of his knees, and to his head and ears. Internally, the air passages were not obstructed, and showed no signs of violence. An examination of his stomach contents revealed partially digested pieces of apple. Dr Dible concluded that drowning had been the cause of death. Dr Millgan testified before the coroner's jury that he and Dr Dible had discovered internal injuries to Tommy which could only have been due to a serious sexual assault having been committed against him, shortly before his death.

Although largely circumstantial, the evidence against Burrows was growing. Tommy's parents confirmed that he had not eaten an apple at home on the morning of his disappearance, and a young lad had been seen eating one in the company of Burrows. That boy had not been positively identified but the police were convinced it was Tommy. There were also the conflicting statements given by him regarding his own movements and those of the deceased. The prosecution now believed they had a motive for the murder, and this had been to prevent Tommy reporting that he had been the victim of a sexual assault by Burrows. On 28 March he was charged with the boy's murder and was committed to appear at the next Derby Assizes.

However, this did not bring an end to police enquiries, for while he was being held in custody for Tommy's murder, an investigation was begun into the disappearance three years earlier of Hannah Calladine, the woman Burrows had married bigamously, and her two children.

Albert Burrows and Hannah Calladine. (Author's collection)

Some years earlier, as the First World War raged in Europe, Burrows who was then forty-six years of age, was working as a fireman at a Cheshire munitions factory. He had left his wife and daughter at the family home in Glossop, and he found lodgings near to his place of work. He was earning a good wage and was able to send money home to his family. He also began an intimate relationship with thirty-eight-year-old Hannah Calladine, a co-worker who lived with her parents, sister and her two-year-old illegitimate daughter Elsie Large, in Nantwich. His wife knew nothing of the relationship with Hannah, just as she was unaware of his family in Glossop. In April 1918 she and Burrows were married at the United Methodist Free Church in Nantwich, and on 26 October that year Hannah gave birth to his son, who was also named Albert.

However, the bigamous marriage was discovered and he was sentenced to six months imprisonment. He was also ordered by the court to pay 7s weekly in maintenance to Hannah. Despite learning the truth about Burrows, Hannah remained fond of him, and in late 1919 she agreed to leave her family home to live with him in Glossop. It was not surprising that his wife, who with her daughter was still living in the family home, refused to tolerate this situation, and she left the house the following day with their child. She applied for maintenance, and on 30 December 1920, Inspector Padwick issued Burrows with a summons to appear before the matrimonial court on 12 January 1920.

A few days before this hearing date, Burrows approached local newsagent George Dale, a friend of his wife's. He asked George to try and persuade her to cancel the court proceedings and return to the family home. He could assure her that the relationship with Hannah was over and she would soon be leaving the house. He said that Hannah had found work as a housekeeper for a single gentleman, who was prepared to allow her two children to live with her in his home.

However, his wife refused his request to cancel the court hearing, which went ahead, and he was ordered to pay her £1 weekly in maintenance. Within days however, his wife and daughter returned to Back Kershaw Street, for just as Burrows had promised Hannah and the two children were no longer living there.

Hannah's family, however, were becoming increasingly worried, as they had received no news from her. They placed advertisements in a number of newspapers, urging her to contact them. They also followed up accounts of her whereabouts given to them by Burrows, but after several weeks, having heard nothing from her, the Calladines contacted the police. Despite being sympathetic and sharing the family's concerns, the police did not have the resources to devote to a full investigation in the absence of any bodies or compelling evidence of a crime having been committed.

Hannah had last been seen with her baby son in her arms at 6.30 p.m. on the evening of Sunday, 11 January 1920 by neighbour Eliza Hammond, who was told by Hannah that they were going for a walk with Burrows. Later that evening, Eliza saw Burrows return alone, and the following day, when questioned by Eliza, he explained that he had taken Hannah and the baby to their new home. He also told Eliza that earlier that day he had taken Elsie to join them, but when Eliza asked where they had gone he replied, 'That is a secret between me and her. I promised I would never tell'.

Earlier in the day at six o'clock in the morning, Burrows had been seen by another neighbour, Margaret Streets, holding Elsie's hand and walking towards Simondley. Two hours later he passed her once again but he was now alone. A few days later she met Burrows and asked him where Hannah and the children were. He told Margaret, 'She has a good job in a relative's bacon shop in Stretford, and we've found a good home for the children'.

For the next three years he continued to give neighbours and the Calladine family the impression that Hannah and the children were still alive. He sent several letters to her parents and sister suggesting they were well. In November 1921, his sister gave birth to a son and Burrows sent a copy of his photograph to Hannah's mother, which was inscribed, 'I send you a photograph of your grandson. I hope you like it'. In another letter he asked Hannah's mother to send him the children's birth certificates, which he needed as they were in hospital recovering from diphtheria.

The police were convinced that Burrows had murdered Hannah and the two children. As for a motive, they believed he had chosen murder as an alternative to paying maintenance. If he had remained with Hannah and the children he would have to pay £1 weekly to his wife and child, and if he remained with his wife and daughter, he would be required to make a weekly payment of 7s to Hannah. He was unemployed without a regular income, and whoever he stayed with, he would face the prospect of prison again for non-payment of maintenance to the other. The police believed he decided to murder Hannah and her children, hoping that his wife would return to the family home, thinking that her rival had left. This would solve his financial worries, as he would have to make no further maintenance payments.

The police discovered that following her disappearance, Burrows had disposed of some of Hannah's belongings. He sold a pram which she had brought with her from Nantwich, to a neighbour Marie Hibbert for 7s and 6d. He also gave one of her coats to Harriet Mellor, from which she made a pair of trousers for her son. That he should dispose of these items, which Hannah would surely have needed in any new home, was another indication that there had been foul play. They became even more suspicious on learning from local jeweller Harold Garside that he had paid Burrows 30s for Hannah's gold wedding ring on 23 February 1920, a possession they thought she would not have willingly got rid off if she was alive.

The police also believed that they knew how he had disposed of the bodies. Following the news of the arrest of Burrows on suspicion of murdering Tommy, and the speculation surrounding the whereabouts of Hannah and the children, Robert Mellor came forward and provided invaluable information. On 19 November 1919, his brother, who was being taken to prison with Burrows, was on Glossop station with a police escort. Robert was also present and heard Burrows, who was about to begin his sentence for failing to pay maintenance to Hannah, tell his brother, 'When I've done my time I'll get this woman. I'll either do her in or put her down the pit shaft.'

The police were convinced that the bodies of Hannah and the children were at the bottom of the disused shaft, in which they had discovered Tommy's body. It was therefore decided to begin a full-scale search of the shaft, and the police team led by Constable Sam Rowe was assisted by a group of volunteer miners from Oldham, under colliery director James Hilton.

The shaft had not been used for more than ninety years, and its crumbling walls meant there was a constant threat of a collapse. Inside the shaft the stench was appalling as for decades, a great deal of farm waste had been dumped in it, and there were many dead animals in various stages of decomposition.

THE WOMAN AND CHILD WERE LAST SEEN NEAR THE PIT SHAFT.

THE MAN WHO FOUND THE REMAINS.

HUMAN BONES AND CLOTHING WERE FOUND.

EXAMINING THE REMAINS

GRUESOME DISCOVERY IN PIT NEAR GLOSSOP.

Following an extensive search of the disused pit, human remains were discovered.
(The Illustrated Police News)

Albert Burrows was subsequently charged with the murder of Hannah Calladine.
(The Illustrated Police News)

The first task was to pump out the water, which was several feet deep at the bottom. However, this proved to be far from straightforward, as the pump which was provided by the local fire brigade broke down frequently. Those working inside the shaft faced constant danger, and on one occasion, part of the timber framework of the windlass, which was used to carry debris to the surface, collapsed. Constable Rowe and miner Thomas Greenwood, who were in the shaft at the time were fortunate to escape unhurt.

Nevertheless, despite the terrible conditions in which they had to work, the police and miners were determined to complete their task, and eventually their tenacity and courage were rewarded. During the afternoon of Wednesday, 23 May, the twelfth day of the search, human remains were found. Dr Burke of Glossop was at the surface ready to provide an initial examination of bones brought from the bottom of the shaft, to determine if they were human. Two small bones, with decomposing flesh still attached to them were confirmed as being part of a baby's forearm, and later that evening, the skull and jaw bone of an older child were recovered.

The search continued for several more days, and the partial skeleton of an adult was formed from a skull, the left side of the pelvis, a thigh bone, several ribs and a shoulder blade. All of the human bones removed from the shaft were examined by Dr J.H. Dible, who confirmed they belonged to an adult female; a female child aged between four and five, and a baby boy. Hannah's family confirmed that she had prominent and distinctive front teeth, which matched those remaining in the woman's skull. This left the police in no doubt as to the identities of the three individuals to whom the remains belonged.

Further evidence came on 1 June, when a pair of clogs was brought to the surface, inside of which were stockings containing the bones of the legs and feet of a young girl. Police enquiries led to the premises of master clogger Philip Robinson of Nantwich, who identified them as a pair he had made to order for Hannah in 1919.

Burrows was committed to Derby Assizes to face trial for the three murders by local magistrates and a coroner's jury in mid-June. His trial took place on 3 and 4 July 1923 before Mr Justice Shearman. Sir Henry Maddocks KC led the prosecution and the defence was led by Norman Winning. He was assisted by Miss G. Cobb, the first female barrister to be briefed in a murder trial in Derbyshire. On the opening day, the defence was taken by surprise by a request from Sir Henry. This was that the cases of Hannah and her children be heard first, and despite the misgivings of the defence, who said they had not had as long to prepare for those cases as they had for that of Tommy's, the judge agreed to the prosecution request.

The Crown called Mrs Hammond and Mrs Streets who had been the last to see Hannah and the children alive over the two day period of 11 and 12 January 1920. Elsie's clogs were identified and Hannah's sister identified her teeth. The financial dilemma facing the accused was also described by Sir Henry. The Crown obviously had a strong case, which was further supported by the evidence of a prisoner who had been with Burrows in the hospital wing of Strangeways Prison during his period on remand awaiting trial.

John Rogers had been serving a short prison sentence and told the court that Burrows asked him, once he was at liberty, to write a brief note addressed to Burrows and send it to him in the prison. He wanted the note to read, 'I and the children are all right. Hope to see you soon'. Burrows wrote several specimen examples of handwriting, supposedly similar to Hannah's, clearly hoping this would persuade others that she had written the note, and that she and the children were still alive. However, his plan failed after Rogers informed prison staff.

The defence attempted to discredit the witness, suggesting he had made the story up so that he might be released early from prison for his cooperation. In reply to a question from the judge, Rogers stated that he had indeed been released fourteen days early, but this was because of his good behaviour throughout his sentence, and was not a reward for giving evidence at the trial.

The defence also argued that the blue woollen dress in which the adult's remains had been found in the shaft, had been sent to Glossop by her family four days after her alleged disappearance and murder at the hands of their client. If the jury accepted this, the Crown's case would fail, as she could not have been murdered on 11 January.

The major plank of the defence case was that Hannah had committed suicide after killing her children. They argued that following the breakdown of the relationship with the accused, and his reconciliation with his wife, she was so distraught that she decided to kill herself. She did so, they claimed, after throwing her children down the shaft to their deaths and then jumping herself. Mr Winning attempted to use the intense public hostility shown towards his client to his advantage, by suggesting that there were several individuals who could support this claim but they were too frightened to come forward for fear of reprisals.

The jury retired for twelve minutes and returned three guilty verdicts. Before passing sentencing the judge asked him if he had anything to say. Burrows replied by saying, 'I am not afraid of death, but I am not guilty. I love those children and the woman too, as true as I hope to meet my God. I am innocent'.

After the condemned man was taken from the dock, the judge ordered the Crown to pay the local authority £363 3s 9d to cover the costs of searching the shaft, in which the bodies had been discovered. He also directed that Burrows should face trial for the murder of Tommy Woods at the next assizes. However, everyone knew that there would be no such trial.

His appeal against conviction was heard before Justices Darling, Slater and Swift, and the defence persisted with the claim that Hannah had committed suicide and argued that there was nothing in the prosecution case that was not consistent with this theory. This was rejected by the court and the appeal failed. Burrows was executed at Nottingham's Bagthorpe Gaol on 8 August by John Ellis, who was assisted by William Willis.

15

A SEVENTY-FIVE-
YEAR-OLD MYSTERY

Ilkeston, 1927

The county's second matricide which led to the gallows occurred in Ilkeston, twenty-two years after John Silk's execution. It was 7 a.m. on 8 February 1927, when William Knighton, a twenty-two-year-old former slaughter man who was then working as a miner, walked into Ilkeston police station to confess to the murder of his fifty-five-year-old mother, Ada Knighton. He asked to speak to Inspector Wheeldon, and in a matter-of-fact voice he told the police officer, 'I have done the old woman in. I have cut her throat with a razor, which is lying at the side of the bed'. The inspector cautioned him, but Knighton continued by saying, 'You'll find it right. I have been on the booze'. The inspector arranged for the man to be detained at the station while he visited the Knighton home at 1 Bethel Street. As he made his way there, Inspector Wheeldon could not have imagined that one of the strangest and most prolonged murder cases of the twentieth century had been set in motion.

On his arrival at the house, he discovered that five people, including the man who had confessed to committing murder, lived there. The suspect's father, George, who because of poor health, slept in the ground-floor living room; William shared a bedroom with his five-year-old nephew, Reginald, on the first floor; and another flight of stairs led to a bedroom in the attic in which Ada and her sixteen-year-old daughter Ivy, shared a bed.

Inspector Wheeldon found Ada's body in her bed with her throat cut. Lying on the floor at the side of the bed, in a pool of blood, was a razor together with its case and a candlestick.

Dr Sudbury arrived at the house and found no other signs of injury or wounds. He later performed a post-mortem and found that death had been caused by the deep wound to her neck, which was 4in long and located just above the Adam's apple. Considerable force had been used in inflicting the wound, which had severed the oesophagus. The doctor confirmed that the razor discovered at the scene had without doubt been the murder weapon. It belonged to George and was always kept in its case in a drawer next to his bed in the downstairs living room, but William had permission to use it whenever he wished to do so.

Ivy had been in the same bed at the time of her mother's death, and she told the police that she had gone to bed at ten o'clock the previous night. Her mother was out at the time, and Ivy did not hear her come to bed. However, at one o'clock in the morning Ivy said she was woken by her mother's coughing. Eventually her mother became quiet and Ivy dropped off to sleep once more. Some time later Ivy woke to discover her brother William, dressed in his shirt and trousers, standing on their mother's side of the bed. Ivy asked him to light a match, and she saw that it was two o'clock. He asked her, 'What's wrong with her Ivy?' to which she replied she did not know. William left the bedroom and Ivy went back to sleep. This however was the first of several differing accounts Ivy was to make about the events in the bedroom that night.

Ada's husband George had been born in 1868, and joined the Army when he was sixteen years old and in which he served for eight years. However, he subsequently re-enlisted and fought in the South Africa campaigns. He left once again but remained a reservist and served in the First World War. He was invalided out of the Army in 1918, and by 1927 he was unable to work due to continuing ill health. He was suffering badly from rheumatism, and twelve months before his wife's death he began to experience chronic heart problems.

He and Ada had raised nine children, but their relationship was not without problems. Ada was a heavy drinker and whenever she came home late and drunk, George, who had a violent temper, would lock her out of the house. When later interviewed by the police, neighbours confirmed that in the six months prior to her death there had been frequent and noisy arguments.

In his interview with the police, William said that he had woken early on the Tuesday morning, dressed, and when he put his hand in his pocket for a cigarette, felt the razor, but he did not know how it had got there. At six o'clock his father shouted upstairs to rouse Ivy and Ada. Ivy got out of bed, dressed and lit a candle. She shook her mother but she did not wake up, and it was then that she noticed the blood on her mother's face and on the floor. She told the police that initially she thought this was the result of a burst blood vessel, and went downstairs where she told William and her father. William went upstairs to his mother's bedroom and came down a few minutes later, telling his father and sister, 'It seems hopeless'.

Ilkeston Town Hall, where William Knighton appeared before the local magistrates. (Author's collection)

George suggested that William take his mother a glass of brandy, which he did. It was as he stood at the side of the bed that he later claimed to have remembered the razor, which he took out of his pocket. Seeing that it was bloodstained, he dropped it with its case to the floor at the side of the bed. He returned to the living room and said that his mother was dead. George told William to fetch his married sister Lois Wake. William said he would do so after he had finished his cup of tea, and after he had done so, he went to his sister's house a few minutes later, and on hearing the news Lois rushed to her parents' home. William told Lois that he was going to see a friend, but instead he went to the police station where he made his confession.

Inspector Wheeldon had questioned Ivy once more on the day following the murder. On this occasion she told him that as she lay in bed on Saturday, 5 February, she had heard William on the stairs outside her bedroom. He had shouted to his mother that he needed some matches, but she had refused to get out of bed. William had then entered the bedroom on his hands and knees and came to Ivy's side of the bed. Ada asked what he was doing, and having replied, 'Nothing', he left the room.

At the time, Ivy's statement seemed to be of no importance to the inspector, but she approached the inspector once again with a different version of events. She said, 'I ought to have told you more yesterday. My brother Billy had connection with me on Saturday night'. She confirmed when questioned further that William had got into bed and had sexual intercourse with her. Their mother, who lay next to them, woke up and William left the bed and crawled quietly out of the room, apparently without Ada having realised what had taken place. Ivy told her mother that there was a man in the room, but did not tell her that it was William. Ada told her not to be silly as there was no one else in the room. Ivy insisted that this was the only occasion that sexual intercourse took place with her brother.

William Knighton's trial took place at the Derby Assizes on Saturday, 26 February 1927 before His Honour Judge Branson. Mr M.F. Healey conducted the prosecution, and the accused was represented by Sir Henry Maddocks KC, who was assisted by Mr T.F. Butler. The defendant pleaded not guilty.

In opening the case for the Crown, Mr Healey advised the jury that suicide had been ruled out, together with the murder having been committed by an unknown intruder. Whoever had committed the crime was in 1 Bethel Street that night, but there was, he admitted, an absence of forensic evidence. The prosecution would be relying heavily on the confession made by the accused, which had been made shortly after the crime had been committed and before the police knew of his mother's death. Furthermore, he had been sober and calm when he entered the police station. Mr Healey proceeded to call his witnesses.

Inspector Wheeldon gave details of the confession, and Dr Sudbury described the results of his post-mortem examination and the cause of death. Lois Wake told the court of her brother calling at her home on the morning of the crime, and of his telling her he was going to see a friend, whereas he went directly to the police station. When asked about William's relationship with his mother, she described it as close and loving.

It was conceded by the prosecution that despite being in bed with her mother at the time of her death, Ivy, who was called as a prosecution witness, had not seen the crime occur. Mr Healey did not raise the issue of her claim to have had sexual intercourse with the accused, and the jury remained unaware of it throughout the trial. It remains unclear why the Crown decided not to raise the matter, as it would have suggested one possible motive for William killing his mother. That is that Ada may have become aware of the fact that her son and daughter were having an incestuous relationship, and possibly in a panic, he killed her to prevent her from revealing this. It may have been that the prosecution felt there was a strong enough case without using this information, given William's unsolicited confession, and possibly felt some sympathy for this sixteen-year-old girl, who had only recently lost her mother in such distressing circumstances, and they wished to avoid embarrassing her publicly by revealing details of the nature of her relationship with her brother. The defence did not raise the matter, as the information would not have helped their client's case. It was clearly to his benefit for the jury to remain unaware of the possibility of any such behaviour.

The accused was an epileptic and Sir Henry called Dr E.W. Morris, a neurologist with the Ministry of Pensions, who testified that in his opinion it was possible for an epileptic when suffering a fit, to cut someone's throat without realising he or she was doing so. Dr Morris stated that at the time of the killing, William's mind could have been deranged so that he would have had no memory of the event. This formed the basis of the defence case and Sir Henry suggested to the jury that the confession by Knighton could be explained. He suggested that having found the bloodstained razor in his pocket, his client immediately presumed he must have committed the crime while he had been having a fit.

William elected to give evidence and insisted that when he found the murder weapon, 'I naturally thought that I must have cut her throat with a razor'. He was cross-examined by Mr Healey, who attempted to discredit this claim:

Mr Healey: And when you saw your mother with the blood lying round her you did not see the wound in her neck?
William: No.

Mr Healey: Therefore there was no reason why you should think that she had not burst a blood vessel?

William: Then I remembered the razor in my pocket. I pulled it out and saw the bloodstains on it and saw all the blood round it and I naturally jumped to the conclusion that I had cut her throat.

Mr Healey: You say 'naturally' but forgive me if I say that was not a natural conclusion to which to come . . .

William: It was because I had blood on my hand here [William indicated the junction of his first finger and thumb on his right hand].

Mr Healey: When you came to the conclusion that you had cut your mother's throat, did you even then go over to look and see whether her throat was cut?

William: No.

Mr Healey: So that, for all you knew when you left the house that morning, you were wrong and her throat had not been cut at all. Is that not so?

William: No. Well, I thought when I found I had got the razor in my pocket and could see I had got blood on my hands, I naturally thought that I had cut her throat.

Mr Healey: And you felt bound to tell the inspector what you knew about the case?

William: Yes.

Mr Healey: Why did you not tell the inspector, 'I have cut my mother's throat. You will find the razor near the bed. I have no recollection about anything.' Why did you not tell the inspector that?

William: I did not think that it had anything to do with the inspector.

Mr Healey: Why did you not say, 'I have no knowledge of doing this at all; I must have done it when I was asleep or unconscious', or something of that sort?

William: I do not know.

In his scrupulously fair summing up, the judge left it open to the jury to return a verdict of guilty but insane, if they felt that the accused had not been fully responsible for his actions, and had cut his mother's throat when in an epileptic state. However, the jury did not agree with this theory and found Knighton guilty of murder, as a consequence of which he was sentenced to death.

On 21 March, Knighton's appeal against his conviction was heard by the Court of Criminal Appeal, before Justices Avory, Shearman and Sankey. It was not admitted by his defence team that he had definitely killed his mother, but they repeated their theory that Knighton might have killed his mother while suffering an epileptic fit, and therefore he could say nothing about the circumstances surrounding her death as he had no recollection of it. They also repeated their claim that his confession to Inspector Wheeldon was understandable given these circumstances.

The appeal was dismissed, and it was pointed out that the defence had called an expert witness to raise this theory, and the judge had specifically left it open to the jury to reach a verdict on the basis of accepting the defence arguments, but this had been rejected by the jury.

One week later, members of the Knighton family approached William's solicitor, Mr Flint. They revealed that since the trial had ended, Ivy had told them of previously unknown details concerning the murder itself, and of her life behind the doors of 1 Bethel Street. She claimed not to have spoken of these matters to anyone before as she was afraid of what her father might do to her in retribution, but she realised that now she must be honest to save her brother from the gallows.

Mr Flint had already been advised by one of the prosecution lawyers at the trial that a medical examination of Ivy had revealed that she was sexually experienced, but this had not been revealed in open court during the trial. Now, Ivy was claiming that she and her father had been engaging in sexual activity since she was twelve years old. Intercourse had never taken place when her mother was in the house, so Ada had remained unaware of what was happening. Ivy told Mr Flint that she now believed that it had been her father who had come into the bedroom on the Saturday night before the murder, and that it was he who had been in the room when her mother was killed. She had not seen his face in the darkness, but claimed to have recognised his cough and the distinctive shuffling sound of his ill-fitting slippers as he climbed the stairs. Ivy further stated that despite her earlier statement she had never been intimate with William.

It was also reported to the police by the family that since the conclusion of William's trial, his father's health seemed much improved, and he had helped paint a room in the family home. The inference was clear, her father was not as disabled as he claimed, and he would have been able to climb the stairs and murder his wife. George Knighton was questioned and agreed that he had tried to help a relative paint a room, but he had soon become extremely tired and had to stop after a matter of minutes. As for the alleged sexual relationship with his daughter, he told the police, 'I am no good to any woman from a sexual point of view'.

Nevertheless, William's execution, which had been set for Thursday, 7 April, was dramatically cancelled by the Home Secretary when Ivy's claims became known to the Crown. For the first time ever, the secretary of state referred a case back to the Court of Appeal for it to be heard again, after it had been dismissed on an earlier occasion. The second appeal was heard before the same judges on Tuesday, 12 April.

The new information was provided partly in person, but largely by written statements. These detailed Ivy's claims to have had an incestuous relationship with her father, and were thus not publicly aired.

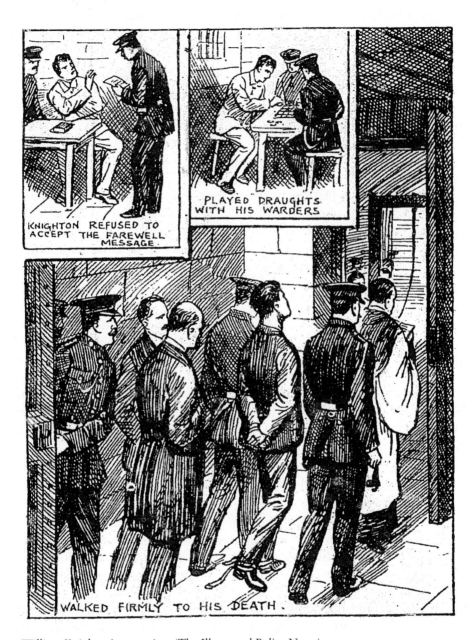

William Knighton's execution. (The Illustrated Police News)

The implications of this revised testimony were clear, namely that it was her father and not William who was the murderer. Implicit in the defence's claims was that George had conducted an incestuous relationship with his daughter for a number of years, murdered his wife when she allegedly discovered this, had allowed his son to take the blame for his crime, and was prepared to see him hang knowing that he was innocent. This scenario was rejected out of hand by the appeal judges, who declared that they did not consider it necessary for George to be called to defend himself against these allegations. The judges were unequivocal in dismissing the appeal and, referring to Ivy's claims, stated:

> We are unanimous that this witness has deliberately given false evidence in her amended statements here, differing from her evidence before the coroner, the Justices, and at the trial. Otherwise we should give the person she has accused an opportunity of denying her charges on oath. The confession made by the appellant on the morning of the murder, when he was calm, sober and explicit stands uncontradicted.

Thomas Pierrepoint officiated at Knighton's execution, which had been rescheduled for 27 April at Nottingham's Bagthorpe Gaol, and which took place without incident. This was despite a petition for a reprieve, which had been well supported in the Ilkeston area.

The inquest into the executed man's death was largely a formality, but Nottingham's coroner, Mr C.L. Botham, took the opportunity of adding his support to the growing movement for an end to capital punishment. He said at the hearing:

> I do not know whether this kind of thing will be likely to continue much longer. The death sentence does not seem to have any deterrent effect. If you notice the newspapers day by day you will see there is a multitude of murders taking place up and down the country. I fancy there is a strong feeling growing for abolishing the death sentence as a policy. I don't know whether we shall have it in our lifetimes, but think the feeling is growing.

Knighton was later buried in the gaol's grounds, and normally that would have been the end of the matter. However, that was not to be the case, as controversy surrounding his conviction and execution would last far beyond even the ending of capital punishment four decades later.

In July 2001, the Knighton case was referred to the Court of Appeal yet again by the Criminal Cases Review Commission (CCRC), which had been established to investigate possible miscarriages of justice. All of the individuals who had played a significant role in the case, be they family members, police officers or lawyers, were dead. However, at the

Thomas Pierrepoint, who hanged Knighton.
(Author's collection)

time of Knighton's execution he had a five-year-old niece, who was now in her eighties. She was deemed to be a person with sufficient interest to want her uncle's memory vindicated, and the CCRC now provided an opportunity for her to attempt to achieve her aim.

On 27 October 2002, Lord Justice Judge, Mr Justice Butterfield, and Mr Justice McCombs sat to hear the appeal, but emphasised that they would not be deciding whether William Knighton had been innocent of the murder, but whether his conviction was safe. They had read the transcripts of the trial and earlier appeals, police files, details of the post-mortem, together with information relating to members of the Knighton family who had been directly concerned in the relevant events.

The judges were quick to raise one issue that puzzled them, and this was the decision of the Crown not to call Ivy to give evidence at the original trial regarding her claim to have had sex with William, which meant that the murder was presented as being essentially motiveless. If Ivy had given such evidence it was, they suggested, reasonable to suppose that the original jury might have considered the possibility that Ada had discovered them together, and in a panic her son had killed her. Nevertheless, they also stated that the decision not to raise this issue was not prejudicial to Knighton's case. Indeed, had it been raised, it may well have made it more difficult for him, and this would explain why the defence did not consider it to be in their client's interests to mention it.

The Old Bailey, where the Knighton case was eventually resolved. (Author's collection)

The judges asked themselves what was new, and they concluded that there was very little. Nevertheless, they agreed to listen to what the CCRC claimed was new evidence. This related to five small spots of blood, which had been found on the stairs leading from the first floor to the attic. This information, it was claimed was suppressed by Inspector Wheeldon, which cast a shadow over the integrity of the whole of his investigation of the crime.

The CCRC had discovered notes made by the inspector at the time, in which he described the stains, which he believed had dripped from a raincoat that had been acting as a cover on the deceased's bed. Lois Wake had told him that she had removed it and taken it to William's room. Unable to prove categorically how the stains came to be on the stairs, it had been decided by the Crown at the time, not to make this a part of their case. Nevertheless, it was clear that the CCRC was wrong in suggesting it was undisclosed evidence, because the stains were raised at the original trial in 1927.

Indeed, the defence attempted to use their existence to help their client as it added weight to his claim to have taken the bloodstained razor out of his mother's room after her death, take it downstairs and return with it later, while in an epileptic daze. The judges drew attention to the following cross-examination of the inspector by Sir Henry on this very point:

Sir Henry: Were there five spots, which you found on the stairs, such as might fall from a dripping razor?
Inspector Wheeldon: Yes, possibly.
Sir Henry: When you found the razor it was upstairs between the shoes?
Inspector Wheeldon: Yes.
Sir Henry: If the razor had been the instrument from which these spots had been dropped by anybody going down it would follow that the razor must have been brought up again.

To the judges this extract demonstrated that as far as they were concerned, Sir Henry had known of the droplets of blood and had attempted to use their presence to Knighton's advantage. They concluded that Inspector Wheeldon had been fair in his handling of this issue and the investigation of the crime as a whole.

On 17 October 2002, the judges again highlighted the huge significance of Knighton's unsolicited confession, when sober, on the morning of the crime, and in a unanimous decision stated:

We have studied all the material drawn to our attention by the CCRC. Having done so, we are troubled that this conviction was referred at all . . . Ultimately, unlike the CCRC, we have been unable to find any significant new information, which on close analysis leads us to doubt the safety of the conviction. Accordingly, the appeal will be dismissed.

This unique case was thus brought to a close after seventy-five years.

BIBLIOGRAPHY

BOOKS

Sharpe, Neville, *The Derbyshire Pit Murders*, 1966
Sutton, John F., *Annals of Crime in the Midlands Circuit; or, Biographies of noted criminals in the counties of Nottingham, Derby, Leicester and Lincoln: From authentic records*, Henry Field (Bookbinder), 1862

NEWSPAPERS

Derby & Chesterfield Reporter
Derby and Derbyshire Gazette
Derby Daily Telegraph
Derby Express
Derby Mercury
The Illustrated Police News

Other titles published by The History Press

Murder & Crime in Lancashire

MARTIN BAGGOLEY

True crime writer Martin Baggoley has selected a fascinating collection of tales of murder and manslaughter from across Lancashire over the last century. The crimes are as diverse as the locations in which they were committed, and include mass murder and suicide in Salford, infanticide in Manchester, robbery and murder in Oldham, a vicious assault over a wager in Liverpool, and rape and murder in Darwen.

978 07524 4358 4

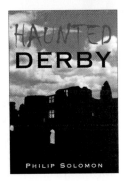

Haunted Derby

PHILIP SOLOMON

Explore the darkest secrets in the history of Derby with this collection of true-life tales from ghost-hunter Philip Solomon. Featuring hooded monks and spectral centurions, the White Lady of Elvaston Castle and a chain-smoking spirit named 'Smokey Joe', his book records all the phantom residents of the ancient city, and provides an intriguing introduction to the hospitals, taverns and streets where 'paranormal becomes normal'.

978 07524 4484 0

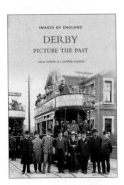

Derby: Picture the Past

SARAH PARKIN AND DARREN HOLDEN

This collection of over 200 old photographssupported by descriptive captions, provide a fascinating pictorial history of some of the buildings, people, transport and memorable events in Derby over a period of more than 150 years. The images include Victorian cityscapes, Derby people at work and leisure, scenes of war and sporting triumph.

978 07524 3580 0

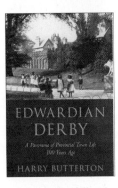

Edwardian Derby

HARRY BUTTERTON

Using local newspapers including the *Derby Mercury*, the *Derby Reporter* and the Derby *Daily Telegraph*, this enthralling volume explores the changes and developments that the Edwardian period brought to Derby. With sections on leisure, industry, crime, religion, education and even the weather, all aspects of daily life in Derby are covered; proving a fascinating glimpse into a lost world.

978 07524 4702 5

If you are interested in purchasing other books published by The History Press, or in case you have difficulty finding any History Press books in your local bookshop, you can also place orders directly through our website
www.thehistorypress.co.uk